Powerful Perspectives on Your Personal World

Powerful Perspectives on Your Personal World

Scripture quotations (except as noted) are from *Today's English Version* (TEV), Copyright 1977, published by Thomas Nelson, Inc.

Scripture quotations marked (TM) are from *The Message,* The New Testament in Contemporary English, by Eugene H. Peterson, Copyright 1993, published by NavPress.

Library of Congress Catalog Card Number: 95-76357
ISBN: 0-9637647-8-0

Powerful Perspectives on Your Personal World

Frank Beall

ARDARA HOUSE, PUBLISHERS
1500 East Johnson Avenue, Suite 123
PENSACOLA, FLORIDA 32514

The theme sculpture, in copper, shown on the front cover, measures about 24" x 24" x 18". It is from the studio of Robert Morgan, an artist who has resided in Waco, Texas, for many years.

My interest in art started early. My mother paid for a few art lessons (fifty cents each, once a week) and at that time kids made many of their own toys. I must have known subconsciously that whatever I did in life would come from my brain through my hands and eyes. I studied dentistry as a profession and began painting along with other art-related activities early in my dental career.

After forty years practicing dentistry I retired and now work in clay, stained glass, copper, and oil paint (palate knife only).

I do only the things that I enjoy and that give me "a better perspective on my personal world."

— Bob Morgan
Waco, Texas
March, 1995

This book is dedicated to my wife, Sylvia, who has been a source of love, support, encouragement, wisdom and inspiration to me for more than three decades.

Preface

Psychiatrist Scott Peck began his best-selling book, *The Road Less Traveled,* with a sentence that is now very familiar to Peck's millions of readers, "Life is difficult." That short three-word sentence seems to be very simple, but it is quite profound because it is so true. Life *is* difficult. It is difficult because it is beset by numerous obstacles and problems, some of our own making, some that are imposed upon us. However life's obstacles and problems come to us, they are real, and we look for help and hope from our faith and other resources.

I have been a Christian all my life. I was raised in a devout Christian home with a strong involvement in the church, and I am grateful to my parents for that heritage. During my high school years I felt a clear call from God to become a minister and I committed myself to that calling when I was seventeen years old. But it was not until I entered the adult world and became a pastor and preacher, devoting my life to relating the Christian gospel to the problems and needs of people in my congregation, that I really came to see that Jesus is the Way, the Truth and the Life. I am convinced that the Christian faith offers us a hopeful and practical perspective on the obstacles and problems that we face in our personal world. The power that makes the perspectives in this book "powerful" is the fact that they are rooted and grounded in the Holy Scripture.

I have been preaching on a regular weekly basis for more than thirty-six years, yet until the publisher approached me about this book, it never occurred to me that my sermons would ever be published in book form. I believe that sermons delivered as a part of worship are one of the means by which God speaks his Word to us. I pray those selected here will become another source of inspiration and faith and hope to those who read them.

I want to thank the patient congregation of Trinity Presbyterian Church in Pensacola, Florida, for the encouragement they have given me for the last quarter of a century.

I am especially grateful to Rebekah Maul, my minister colleague, and others on our staff for their love and support.

Most of all, I want to thank my thoughtful and wise wife, Sylvia, to whom this volume is dedicated. For more than thirty-one years she has been a much needed, steadying influence for me, enriching my life beyond words. She and I are the fortunate and proud parents of two wonderful children — now productive adults — Charles and Angela, and I am thankful for the joy that they have given us. I appreciate, as well, the love that I receive from them and their spouses, Paige and Cyrus.

Frank Beall
Pensacola, Florida
February, 1995

Contents

1

Bad Luck
and
Broken Dreams

When a young man, he went to the Black
Hawk War as a captain and, through no fault of his
own, returned a private. He then went into a small
business but a worthless partner put him into
bankruptcy. He fell deeply in love with a girl, but
she died. He was a mediocre lawyer in a little
midwestern town — too impractical, too unpol-
ished, too temperamental to be a success. He was
defeated in his first try for the legislature, defeated
in his first attempt to be nominated for congress,
defeated in his application to be Commissioner of
the General Land Office, defeated in the senatorial
election of 1854, defeated in his efforts to be vice

president in 1856, and defeated again in the senatorial election of 1858. He sought to be a lyceum lecturer — but failed. After he was elected to the presidency of the United States in 1861, many people considered him to be a failure. He was killed by an assassin's bullet. But historians generally regard Abraham Lincoln to be one of our nation's best presidents in spite of his failures.

Americans worship success so much that failure is considered to be almost un-American. Millions of us are being victimized by the success syndrome.

I am sure that my experience in this regard is typical of others my age. From the time I was very young my father said to me repeatedly: "I want you to be the best in whatever you do. Even if you're a crook, be the best one. Never settle for second best." I was always pressured to make top grades in school and to excel in other activities, and, as many of my parishioners know, I am still a rather competitive person.

While there may be people who lack ambition and motivation, most of us want to be successful in our work and our relationships, and we try to instill in our children a desire to succeed. In fact, we take such pride in our children's success that their success makes us feel successful.

A part of the adventure in pursuing success, of course, is the risk of failure. If there were no possibility of failure, some of the lustre of success would be tarnished. For many people the fear of failure is the primary motivation to succeed.

Each of us fails at something. Even those who are the most successful in the public's eye have their private failures. Many people who are recognized for their success in their business or professional lives have failed in some other area. Every day we read of major business executives — Donald Trump comes to mind — who are spectacularly successful in business or other activities but who do not have a clue about how to relate to a wife or raise a child. Many CEOs in major corporations balance their business and personal family lives well, but many of them also neglect their spouses and children and fail in those relationships.

Failure is a reality of life. No one succeeds at everything. All of us have experienced failure to some extent in one area or another of our lives. In school. In work. In family relationships. In some personal moral ways. In ways we have not even considered.

Because experience of failure is universal, we can relate to Simon Peter in his experience. The Gospel of John tells the story of his failure as a follower of Jesus. At one point, when Jesus knew that his death was imminent, he predicted that Peter would deny him. In the accounts of Matthew, Mark, and Luke, Peter emphatically protested that even if all the other disciples of Jesus denied him, he would never do so. But Jesus knew that he would.

"Where are you going, Lord?" Simon Peter asked him.

"You cannot follow me now where I am going," answered Jesus; "but later you will follow me."

"Lord, why can't I follow you now?" asked Peter. "I am ready to die for you!"

Jesus answered, "Are you really ready to die for me? I tell you the truth: before the rooster crows you will say three times that you do not know me."

John 13:36-38
(Read also John 18:15-27; 21:15-19)

It was only a short time later, after Jesus was arrested and was being interrogated by various religious and political leaders, when the atmosphere was obviously quite tense, that Peter began to feel insecure about his own safety. He tried to mingle among the soldiers and guards and other bystanders to hide himself. When he was asked if he was one of Jesus' disciples, Peter blurted out, "No, I am not." Two more times he was asked if he was a follower of Jesus and both times Peter denied it. Immediately afterwards, Jesus was taken to trial, was sentenced to death, and was eventually beaten and crucified on a cross as a common criminal.

Certainly Peter did not set out to fail. Before, when he was removed from the pressure of the occasion, when Jesus predicted that he would deny him, Peter had insisted that he would not. When we are safely removed from a pressure situation, we do the same thing. We're confident that we can handle the stress and the pressure, so we go into the fray. Actually, our chances for success are increased if we believe up front that we can succeed. But sometimes in the heat of the battle, in the intensity of the difficult moment, we find that the pressure is too great and we buckle under it. Sometimes we take the path of least resistance and compromise. We panic. We lose our composure. Sometimes we lose our moral principles. In any or all of those cases we fail, and often the guilt and the embarrassment can be devastating.

As devastating as failure is, that need not be the end of the story. Abraham Lincoln's experience is a case in point and so is Simon Peter's. We can rise from each failure and move on to successes. Indeed, the person who succeeds is not the one who holds back, fearing failure, nor the one who never fails but rather the one who moves on in spite of failure.

I have devised several steps that have helped me when I have failed.

15

❖

First is to do a thorough, honest self-examination in order to take responsibility for my actions instead of blaming other people and circumstances. We know very well that some enterprises cannot succeed because they are in the wrong place at the wrong time. We know that some people are impossible to live with. We know that some moral pressures are extremely overwhelming. We also know that most of the time we have our own parts to play in the failure. If we insist on blaming other people and adverse circumstances, we can learn nothing about ourselves. But if we are willing to examine ourselves and to face up to our own responsibilities, then there are things that we can learn that will help us to make changes and improvements in the future.

Next is a reevaluation of what personal success means. Excellent guidelines for this exercise are found in Ralph Waldo Emerson's reflections on success.

How do you measure success?

To laugh often and much;

To win the respect of intelligent people
  and the affection of children;

To earn the appreciation of honest critics
  and endure the betrayal of false friends;

To appreciate beauty;

To find the best in others;

16

> To leave the world a bit better
> whether by a healthy child,
> a redeemed social condition,
> or a job well done;
> To know even one other life has breathed
> because you lived —
> this is to have succeeded.

Reflecting on Emerson's comments, Chuck Swindoll says, "I'm impressed. I appreciate what isn't mentioned as much as what is. Emerson doesn't once refer to money, status, rank, or fame. He says nothing about power over others, either. Or possessions. Or a super-intimidating self-image. Or emphasis on size, numbers, statistics, and other visible nonessentials in light of eternity."[1]

An effective way to get serious about a reevaluation is to write down a personal mission statement which explicitly states the desired accomplishments. My own Statement of Success includes being faithful in using my talents and in serving others in the name of Christ.

We must realize that though we fail, we are not failures. We are made by God in his likeness. We are known and loved by God from eternity and for eternity. Therefore we are of infinite worth. It is very important that we separate the fact that we occasionally fail from the self-concept that says we are failures. In a time of failure, it is important to say, "I failed, but I am not a failure. I am a child of God and I am loved by God."

The next step necessary in getting beyond failure is to accept God's forgiveness for failure. Jesus forgave Peter and accepted him. The following dialogue between Peter and Mary after the resurrection is suggested in *This Fleeting Instant* by Joe Elmore:

Simon Peter:
>Mary, did he really call my name?
>You're sure? You couldn't have misunderstood
>>him? He said my name?

Mary Magdalene:
>Yes. Peter, I distinctly heard him.
>He said "Peter" as clearly as you hear me now.

Simon Peter:
>What was the tone of his voice?
>Was he angry — did you hear anger toward me?
>Did he sound like he wanted to see me so he
>>could . . . well, you know what I did.

Mary Magdalene:
>He spoke with kindness, Peter.
>In fact, he paused when he said your name.
>I noticed a tenderness in his face —

18

the same tenderness I remember
the many times he held children on his lap.
*Peter bows his head, stunned, then falls to his knees
and weeps.*
Simon Peter:
Dear God!
I thought I would never hear my name called
again, except in shame.[2]

The tremendous significance of this forgiveness made the difference to Peter between giving up in failure or persevering to become a significant force for God.

Walter Underwood wrote: "It would have been impossible for Peter to preach that marvelous sermon at Pentecost where three thousand were added to the church, had he been carrying in his conscious mind the memory of his shameful denial of Jesus Christ. Indeed, we must forget our failures and accept God's forgiveness if we are to press forward to success in the future."[3]

God's forgiveness is always there for us to receive. In a time of failure we can accept his forgiveness and move on. What joy there is in not clinging to unnecessary guilt!

The final step is to let God lead beyond failure to new opportunities. Jesus singled Peter out, called him aside, checked out his love and devotion and gave him new responsibilities. There are always doors opening to new opportunities. The new opportunities might be very different from our previous experiences, but in God's ever changing world, there is always something else that we can do. The secret is to be open to the leadership of the Holy Spirit and willing to move in new directions.

For Peter the opportunity came in the formation of the church. Without Peter's leadership following the death of Jesus, would Christianity have become the force it is in the world today? Perhaps Peter, as he watched the growth of the church, would sometimes think of the second chance Christ gave to him.

The God who is revealed in Jesus, the God whom we worship and serve, is a God of new beginnings. His love for us is so strong and his forgiveness is so sure that we can view our failures as temporary. We can turn them over to him and leave them there and, under his guidance, rise up and start over again.

2

Power,
Love,
and Self-control

*For the Spirit that God has given us does not
make us timid; instead his Spirit fills us with
power, love, and self-control.*

II Timothy 1:7

The words from the scripture are words of encouragement that the veteran Apostle Paul wrote to Timothy, his young colleague in the ministry, who could
anticipate some rough times ahead. Society as a whole
was not warm to the new Christian movement. Life
was hard. Travel and living conditions were poor for
the early leaders of the movement. But Paul and
Timothy surely saw their journeys as a great adventure,
even if a fearful one. Paul Tournier, the Swiss author
and physician, understood about fear and adventure.

21

The adventurous life is not one exempt from fear, but on the contrary one that is lived in full knowledge of fears of all kinds, one in which we go forward in spite of our fears. Many people have the utopian idea that others are less afraid than they are, and they feel therefore that they are inferior. All men are afraid, even desperately afraid. If they think they are exempt from fear, that is because they have repressed their fears. Fear is part of human nature.[4]

Fear is one of the most useful and, at the same time, one of the most destructive of all human emotions. It is a powerful motivator for safety and improvement. Fear can motivate us to marshal our resources to meet a crisis satisfactorily. It helps us to make plans for the future so that we will not be caught unprepared by some possible disaster. Every year the officials at the Naval Air Station in Pensacola spend a good bit of time and money going through a mock hurricane drill to make sure that they will be prepared when a real hurricane comes this way. That wise action is prompted by a healthy fear of hurricanes. So are many of the routine actions we perform each day. Dr. Cecil Osborne writes:

Fear of consequences prompts us to obey the traffic signal almost automatically. The consequence could be either an accident or a police citation. Fear of hunger prompted the cave man to go in search of meat, and it sends modern man forth to his job. Fear of ending one's days in want prompts one to save for the future and to invest with caution. Fear of failure and consequent shame or disapproval usually causes the student to keep his grades up. In a week's time a typical person may take hundreds of actions which are prompted by some instinctual fear.[5]

Such fears play a part in the development of self-discipline, which can be very valuable. Other fears, though, can be extremely powerful, destructive, and debilitating. The most serious kind of fear, of course, is what is known as a phobia, which is defined as a fear "that exceeds normal proportions and that has no basis in reality." Many different phobias often require professional help to overcome. There are more "normal" fears with which most of us contend from time to time. They might not be obsessive or irrational like phobias, yet they cause us anxiety, sometimes with crippling effects.

Fear of failure can keep us from risking or even trying. Fear of personal inadequacy can make us withdraw from others or at least keep us from reaching out to befriend others or to seek out new opportunities. My congregation may see me as quite gregarious, but when I was in my late teens and twenties I was fearful about asking girls to go on dates. I used to envy those guys who would walk right up to unknown but attractive girls and ask them for a date. I never could do that and I always used to get angry at myself because I couldn't. Fortunately, when I met Sylvia — now my wife — I didn't have to rely on any special technique! It was a joyous and spontaneous event.

Fear of death — our own, or the loss of loved ones — and fear of the future, especially as it relates to job and economic security, can be debilitating. A relatively new one is fear of old age. Thanks to the advances of medical science, we are living longer and many of us fear a crippling old age when we will lose control of our physical and mental capacities and become a burden to others and to ourselves.

Some fears may be linked to specific events or activities. A spouse is unfaithful. A growth within the body is malignant. An accident occurs when loved ones are traveling. Other fears are born of imagination. Such fears stifle our energy and creativity.

Sometimes fear creates what we fear. The fear of failure, for example, can keep us from risking and can immobilize us so that we do fail. The fear of personal inadequacy can make us ineffective. The fear of economic insecurity can lead us to make unwise investments or business decisions. The fear that a spouse is having an affair can drive that spouse into a relationship with another person. In all of these examples fear, which can often be helpful, becomes counterproductive.

Our emotions affect our bodies in such a way that fear can affect our physical health. When I become excessively fearful or anxious, I get a headache and a tightening in the stomach and have difficulty sleeping. I can see how prolonged stress of that kind can lead to stomach ulcers or high blood pressure.

Though there is good reason to be thankful for and to respect the healthy fears that protect us and motivate us to improve, we need to deal with and overcome those fears that stifle growth and creativity and actually harm us physically, mentally, emotionally, and spiritually. I have found that our Christian faith offers us an antidote to fear. God has given us in the Second Letter to Timothy a gift that speaks directly to our battle against crippling fear: *For the Spirit that God has given us does not make us timid; instead his Spirit fills us with power, love, and self-control.*

Some scholars would argue that the word "Spirit" here does not refer to the Holy Spirit, the third person of the Trinity, but to a kind of Spirit that is like school spirit or team spirit. Yet others argue that "Spirit" here is not native to human beings and is not an achievement — that is, something we work up or produce. It is God's gift. It is, therefore, God's Spirit.

I personally contend, and Christian experience verifies over and over again, that just as the Holy Spirit came to those early disciples and empowered them, so the Spirit of God comes to us and gives us the power to overcome our fears.

The word "power" in the scripture means boldness or courage, a confidence bolstered by the work and ministry of Jesus Christ. We Christians believe that in Jesus we see what God is like and that God is love and that the world and all of us in it are in the hands of a loving God. In times of trouble others might believe the world is in the hands of an unfeeling, uncaring, vindictive God or fate, but we know and believe that even in dark times we are in the hands of a loving, caring God.

Christians also believe that, in his death and resurrection, Christ has defeated even death, thus freeing us to face whatever happens in the future with courage and confidence. Knowing and believing in what Jesus has accomplished and holding him in our hearts, we are given power which makes us adequate for anything that happens.

After power, Paul mentions a second promise: *God's Spirit fills us with love.* It is good that we are given the Spirit of love because power, pure naked power, by itself is always dangerous and corrupting. Love becomes a channel to power in that it directs attention away from self toward others. Fear comes from what we perceive are threats to the self. Fear is, therefore, an unhealthy self-centeredness. Love, it has been well said, "is self-denial and self-surrender, outgoingness from self into life and people and God. Love then casts out fear because it casts out unhealthy self-consciousness."

John expresses this idea when he writes in I John 4:18 that *There is no fear in love; perfect love drives out all fear.*

The third promise, Paul reminds Timothy (and us!), is that *God's Spirit gives us self-control.*

Possibly Paul wanted to protect Timothy from fanaticism, from courting martyrdom for its own sake. Some people who have overcome their timidity will plunge into excesses of religion and even fanaticism. Self-control "suggests moderation, a temperate mind, the opposite of extremism of all kinds." Sometimes even love needs some self-control and self-discipline. Love has limits and sometimes needs to be what we call "tough." Love sometimes has to discipline and love sometimes has to let go. The boldness and outgoing love that come through the Spirit gift must be tempered by self-control.

In one short sentence the old apostle gives the young Timothy the keys that can unlock for him the secrets to success in his ministry. Those same keys can open for us the door to lives lived without crippling fear. If we are "timid" and feel inadequate to face life's battles, we have the promise of an unending supply of enabling resources: power, love, and self-control.

3

Stress,
Fatigue,
and Depression

Most men live
lives of quiet desperation.
— Henry David Thoreau (1817-1862)

John Gray is at the most productive period of his professional career. He is vice president in charge of marketing for his company. Sales have reached an all-time high. His company has rewarded him with pay increases and bonuses. His community recognizes his success and abilities and calls upon him often for leadership on boards and projects. John has a lovely wife who also has her own career and is fulfilled in it. The two of them are compatible and close. Their children are bright and attractive and have always been leaders and models of good behavior. One of them is in graduate school and the other is in college, and both seem to have promising careers ahead of them.

In spite of all that, for several weeks John has been listless and despondent. He is tired all the time and can hardly get through the day. Some days getting up and going to work takes all the strength he can muster. Sometimes he just muddles through the day. He is smart enough to realize that if things do not change quickly, his relationship with the corporation will begin to go sour. When he gets home at night, he doesn't feel like talking to his wife or going anywhere. He just wants to go to bed and sleep it off. He is concerned that the one drink that he used to have before dinner has been stretched to two and sometimes three.

Sally Jones is known in her community as a pathfinder because she is one of the first women in her town to make it in a profession that has been regarded as reserved for men. Because of her competency and tenacity, she has paid her dues and demonstrated that she can compete with anyone. People wait in line for her services. She, too, has a fulfilling marriage. People have marveled at how well she has been able to be a good homemaker and mother to their high-achieving children. But lately she has been drained of energy. She has been getting to work later and later and finds herself canceling appointments more and more. Her husband and children and office colleagues have been noticing that she is becoming more irritable and short-tempered. She only nibbles at her food, has lost weight and, in general, has become more careless about her appearance. But even worse, she doesn't seem to care much about how she functions and relates to other people.

Bob Evans stands near the top of his senior class and is an officer in a number of activities in his high school. He has a steady girl friend who is a cheerleader and was also Homecoming Queen. Bob is getting ready to take his college entrance exams and shows promise of being able to get into his choice of colleges. But lately, for some reason unknown to him, he is losing interest in his studies and activities and is beginning not to care how well he does on the SAT. Some call it "Senioritis" but he doesn't think so. He seems to have less energy and ambition and, for some strange reason, he is becoming irritable and abrasive.

On the surface, John and Sally and Bob all seem to have it made in life. They are all competent and physically healthy people. They are blessed with material comforts and enjoy the love of their families and the respect of their communities. Certainly they have everything that a person should need to feel happy and content. But they feel despondent, discouraged, and downcast. They are lacking in life and energy. If things are going so well for them, why do they feel so bad?

John, Sally, and Bob are all suffering from what we call "burn-out." Sometimes we describe persons with such difficulties as being "stressed out." Whatever we call it, intense stress or pressure can go on so long that it begins to get the best of those experiencing it. It saps our strength and energy. It blocks our desire to keep going and makes us want to quit.

Apparently this is not a new problem for humans. The prophet Elijah experienced a crisis something like my fictional friends John and Sally and Bob did. The Lord worked with Elijah to bring him out of it, and I believe that there are things that we can learn from his experience that can help us.

Elijah was a person who seemed to "have it all together." He had become known throughout Israel as a powerful prophetic figure. He had the courage to confront even the powerful King Ahab and Queen Jezebel about their wrong-doing! On one occasion, when a widow's son apparently died, Elijah applied what seemed to have been a form of mouth-to-mouth resuscitation and prayed fervently for his recovery, and the boy was brought back to life.

More familiar to us is his confrontation with the prophets of Baal on Mount Carmel. This great story in I Kings 19:1-21 has elements of humor and high drama. On that occasion Elijah challenged Ahab the King and all four hundred and fifty prophets of Baal and the four hundred prophets of Asherah to meet him on Mount Carmel. Then Elijah arranged a contest. The prophets of Baal would take a bull, kill it, cut it in pieces, put it on an altar with wood (to make it burn better), and he would do the same with another bull. Then the prophets of Baal would pray to their god to light the fire, and he would pray to his God to light his fire. And the god who answered by setting the bull on fire would be declared the real god. When the Baal prophets prepared their bull, they prayed to their god until noon, but no answer came. All the while Elijah taunted them: "Pray louder! Maybe he is daydreaming. Perhaps he has gone off on a trip. It could be that he is asleep. Wake him up!" But no answer came even though they continued to plead all day long.

Then Elijah prepared his bull, and, to make things more dramatic and to make it harder for his God to set the fire, he poured water on the bull and the wood. At the hour of the afternoon sacrifice, Elijah approached the altar and quietly prayed:

> *O Lord, the God of Abraham, Isaac and Jacob, prove now that you are the God of Israel and that I am your servant and have done all this at your command. Answer me, Lord, answer me, so that this people will know that you, the Lord, are God and that you are bringing them back to yourself.*
>
> I Kings 18:36,37

We are told that *the Lord sent fire down, and burned up the sacrifice, the wood and the stones, scorched the earth and dried up the water in the*

33

trench. When the people saw this, they threw themselves on the ground and exclaimed, *"The Lord is God; the Lord alone is God."*

And then all the prophets of Baal were killed.

Now, we might think that after being the instrument for bringing a widow's son back to life and after the dramatic and decisive victory over the 450 prophets of Baal, Elijah would have been on top of the world. But, alas, he was not. Instead, he immediately sank into the pits of despondency and despair. To be sure, Queen Jezebel had threatened to take revenge by killing him, but Elijah had never before felt intimidated by the wrath of anybody, even an unusually powerful monarch. I'm not discounting fear as a factor, but I have to believe that he was overloaded with intense, unrelenting stress and pressure that finally got the best of him.

This is not to say that pressure is all bad. Some degree of urgency, some stress, is essential. A fine concert piano has 243 strings, so taut they effect a 40,000 pound pull on the piano's frame. Without that stress the piano would not play in tune. As human beings, we too need some stress. But each of us must discover the appropriate amount of pressure because too much stress is dangerous.

In this wonderful account from I Kings 19 we discover that Elijah had a case of discouragement and despair. No wonder! He had dealt with Ahab's evil reign over Israel, with severe drought, with the priests of Baal, and finally with Jezebel on a rampage. First, he ran away from his problems. Then, along the way he became suicidal. Stopping under a tree to rest, the record says that Elijah *"wished he would die"* and actually prayed, *"It's too much, Lord. Take away my life: I might as well be dead."*

When we start feeling so hopeless that we think death is the only alternative — that death is to be preferred over life — life can hardly be any more bleak.

Until recently, a minister might deal with self-inflicted deaths only once in a decade. Now this tragedy occurs much more often in any given period. It has become even more familiar to every pastor. "Suicide, the ultimate rejection of one's self, plays no favorites and knows no limit. In my files and memory," writes Charles Swindoll, "are unforgettable cases that span the extremes: a successful banker, a disillusioned divorcee, a run-away, the son of a missionary, a mother of three, a wealthy cartoonist, a professional musician, several collegians, a Marine, a retired grandfather, a medical doctor, a middle-aged playboy, a brilliant accountant, a growing number of teens who were in junior and senior high schools. These individuals struggled with feelings of loneliness, worthlessness, insecurity, a lack of hope, intense perfectionism, alienation from meaningful relationships, and a tragic sense of feeling unloved and unlovely."[6]

Elijah, after running away and suffering suicidal feelings, revealed another common symptom of intense unrelenting pressure: self-pity. He said to God:

> *Lord God Almighty, I have always served you — you alone. But the people of Israel have broken their covenant with you, torn down your altars, and killed all your prophets. I am the only one left — and they are trying to kill me.*

When things begin to look bleak and hopeless, and our world seems to be crumbling around us, we tend to feel that we are all alone. It's hard to believe that anyone else cares about what happens to us or could help us even if they did care.

The powerful, charismatic prophet Elijah, in the aftermath of two dramatic successes, found himself in deep despair, feeling suicidal and wallowing in self-pity. It is interesting to see how God dealt with him at that low point and pulled him out of his desperate condition. There are things that we can learn from this incident that will serve us well when we are down.

First, Elijah slept. He was not only emotionally drained, he was physically exhausted, too, so he rested. We all need to remember this wise adage for athletes: Listen to your body. When fatigue or pain sets in, it is time to rest and let the body recuperate. After Elijah slept, he was awakened by an angel and told to eat and drink. He needed nourishment if his body was to recuperate. Often when we are down, we neglect our physical needs. Granted, when we are despondent, sometimes we are not hungry and we feel too keyed up to sleep and rest, but we need to eat something anyway and we need to try to rest, as well, or things could be worse later.

When Elijah had rested and eaten, the Lord led him up to Mount Sinai, the place where Moses received the Ten Commandments, and in many ways the place of Israel's spiritual roots. It was a journey back to spiritual basics, back to those things that could serve to renew his faith.

After physical rejuvenation each of us needs to get back to spiritual basics. Years ago the Alban Institute published a paper for ministers on how to be rejuvenated, contending that many ministers begin to suffer "burn-out" after ten years. I had been in my present pastorate about fifteen years at that point, and though I didn't feel really burned-out, I ordered the paper. I was glad I did, for I found several helpful ideas in it that I believe have helped my ministry and, indeed, my personal health. Among other things emphasized was the need to renew one's spiritual vitality. A part of this renewal is to maintain the proven spiritual disciplines of prayer and meditation. I found that following that course more diligently was indeed helpful in renewing my spiritual energy and purpose.

37

Sometimes we need to devise techniques to accomplish diligence. In a new book, *Prayer-Walking,* Linus Mundy writes that praying and walking go together naturally. He suggests five steps:

1. Retreat: Get away physically from the house, the office, the telephone.
2. Rethink: Notice the world around you, the world you do not see from the house or the car.
3. Remember: Reflect on memories, good and bad, all the way back to childhood.
4. Repent: See new directions, new choices in life.
5. Repeat: To continue the benefits, do it often.[7]

Mundy attests to benefits gained with walking at any pace from leisure walking to power walking. Biking, too, gives a new view, providing a physical work-out and a renewal of spirit.

Prayer, when combined with exercise, can take many forms, from formal prayers to meditation on a sentence or a phrase. A line from a psalm, a sentence from scripture, a phrase from a remembered prayer — all provide fruitful sources for prayer exercise.

"One thing I have discovered," writes the noted Swiss physician and author Paul Tournier, "is the great psychological value of meditation. . . . In the profound atmosphere of meditation we become conscious of the real and hidden motives of our feelings, our desires, our fears, and our emotions."

He tells about a conversation he had with a young woman who said,

"When a woman gets married she is like a work when the copyright has run out — she belongs to her family, to society, to anybody; she has no more privacy." She added that her own private refuge was her bathroom. And why not? For my part [continues Tournier], I find I can meditate in the anonymity of a restaurant, where I am safe from the telephone but surrounded by the buzzing, busy world in which I want to be present. Sometimes, instead of spending one's holidays devouring distances or rushing from one museum to another, one can spend whole days meditating in the silence of meadow or wood, or in a monastery. The busier we are, the more do we become burdened with responsibilities, and the more do we stand in need of these times when we can renew our contact with God.[8]

After God led Elijah to rest, to nourish his body, and to renew his spirit, God reminded Elijah that he was not in fact alone, that there were plenty of others who were still on the Lord's side. Indeed, he told Elijah that he had seven thousand loyal people in Israel, people who had not turned away to follow Baal.

39

In down periods it is easy to feel that we are alone. I suppose there are times when we are, but most of us have family and friends who care about us, and I'm amazed at all the community and church support groups available for almost every human need. My feeling is that there are almost always people nearby who are willing and ready to provide support. We may need to take a step toward them, though, to receive it. While we stumble around, yearning for that external support, let us remember that we have an internal support system that can help us to reach out — the Divine Companion, who is always with us.

The classic story to illustrate how reaching out brings support is the story of a businessman named Bill. Intelligent and competitive, he was also very lonely. He had drunk himself out a job. When he became an alcoholic, he worked hard at conquering his drinking habit — and thought he had. In the nineteen-thirties, on a business trip to Akron, during too much lonely free time on a weekend afternoon, he became obsessed with the desire to drink. Realizing that the cycle would start all over again, he struggled.

He dialed all the church numbers he could find in the local directory, and when a clergyman answered he said — not knowing quite why — that he was a "rumhound from New York" who needed "to speak now with another alcoholic." He ended up visiting a local surgeon named Bob Smith, who was known around town as a hopeless boozer; and their encounter was, in effect, the first A.A. meeting. . . . It took a while for the two men to identify the "stuff" that had saved them: the therapeutic value for oneself of helping another person stay sober. . . . They began to visit patients in detox, telling their story, and inviting them to give the new therapy a try.[9]

These men have proved that helping somebody else is a valid part of our external support system, of our recovery from despair. When we are depressed and despondent, we need some way to get our minds off ourselves and find a sign that there is promise for the future. I cannot spell out how helping another works for each individual person, but I do know that when we step outside ourselves to help others, our despondency lifts and our problems begin to shift into perspective. Then new opportunities usually appear.

Elijah and his story tell how stress, fatigue and depression may be helped. More than three thousand years later, when feeling burned out or despondent, whether or not things are otherwise going well, we can remember Elijah's experience. From it we can learn how to live fully again. Take care of physical needs. Return to those basic disciplines that aid spiritual renewal. Remember that others have been there and can help.

Look for opportunities to get outside one's self by helping others. And look for signs of future hope.

4

Patience, Kindness, Envy, and Selfishness in the Family

I believe that the simplistic old saying, "The family that prays together stays together," has some truth to it, but at the same time I believe that strong families need more. It is not a trite truism to say that contemporary families need all the help they can get. It was never simple, even though it used to seem so.

Professors Nick Stinnett of the University of Alabama and John DeFran of the University of Nebraska did a survey of three thousand strong families in several countries, including several ethnic groups, and published their results in a book entitled *Secrets of Strong Families.*

The survey resulted in a listing of six important factors:

Strong families are committed to the family.
Strong families spend time together.

Strong families have good family communication.

Strong families express appreciation to each other.

Strong families are able to solve problems in a crisis.

Strong families have a spiritual commitment.[10]

I am convinced that the secret of the strongest families is the reinforcement, through the Christian faith, of these qualities that Stinnett and DeFran mention. As I listed them, I immediately thought of the characteristics or qualities of love that Paul describes in his love chapter, I Corinthians 13.

First, love is patient.

Patience is not one of my virtues, but — thank goodness for our family — it is one of my wife Sylvia's strong points, and through the years I have begun to learn some things about it from her example to me.

The Old Testament records several times when even God's patience was sorely tried! But holding the story together is the pattern of his long-suffering patience with the people of Israel. Across the centuries millions of people have ignored him and have even been hostile toward him. If I were in his place, I fear I would have destroyed the world long ago!

Jesus' patience with people set the perfect example for us. He was very patient with the disciples when they failed to understand what he was about. He was patient with the religious leaders who understood even less and issued challenges at every turn. He was patient with the multitudes who made constant demands on him! Jesus was never too busy, too impatient to listen and to learn what was going on in the lives of persons he encountered in the most casual way.

Sociologist and lecturer Tony Campolo in his book *Carpe Diem* recounts an experience which deeply affected his own relationship with people, including his family.

Once, some years ago, a student came to my office after a lecture and asked me a rather perfunctory question. As he sat there asking me something about some theory I had expounded in class, I was a bit impatient. I had other things I had to do. He could have looked up the answer himself, and I was really a bit too busy right then to give him any real quality time.

That young man left my office, returned to the high-rise apartment house where he lived, went up to the roof, and jumped to his death. His life was snuffed out less than twenty minutes after he had left me.

I was the last one to ever talk to that young man. I now realize that when he came to my office, it wasn't to ask a question about sociology, but to cry out for help. He had heard me speak with passion about love during class and probably had been led to believe that I cared for him. He reached out, and in my busyness I heard only what he said. I did not hear his feelings. I missed the cry for help that often comes over and under the words of troubled people. I failed to hear what this young man meant; I did not grasp what he could not put into words. Jesus would have done better.

What I failed to do for that young man I find that husbands and wives often fail to do for each other; they don't stop everything else when it's time to listen and pay attention to each other's souls. So many married people do not seem to understand how important it is to regularly take time to feel these groanings that cannot be uttered. (See Romans 8:26)[11]

How different life in our families would be if we could take just a little more time with each other, if we had Jesus' patience, his tolerance, his understanding, his compassion for others who do not do things the way we think they should or when we think they should!

Paul's description of love as "patient" is quickly followed with "Love is kind." Indeed, he speaks of love as *patient* and *kind* in one sentence. To be patient suggests self-restraint, while to be kind suggests the overt expression of that love to someone else. In family life we often need to be long-suffering and tolerant, but those traits are not enough; we often need to be actively kind.

Families thrive on actual deeds of unsolicited kindness. At the minimum, healthy family life calls for every member to carry his or her share of the load, but family life is further enhanced by thoughtful deeds that help others and that demonstrate affection and caring.

This poignant story about a child's experience was told to me several years ago.

Her Uncle Jack would come from out of town occasionally to visit her family and she looked forward to his visits because every time he followed the same affectionate ritual. He would call Jill over, smile, wink, take a quarter from his pocket, put it in her hand, pick her up and hug and kiss her. Once, however, when Uncle Jack came for a visit, though he was nice, there was no wink or smile, no quarter or hug. Jill was convinced that Uncle Jack did not love her any more.

Her mother sensed Jill's disappointment and took her aside, pointing out that Uncle Jack was no longer working, had few quarters to spare, and was short himself on feeling needed and useful. Then she said to Jill, "Why don't you go to him this time with a wink and a hug and a kiss?"

"I did," Jill recalled, "and he hugged me back very hard. Boy, I felt terrific! I knew I had given him something he needed very much — love from me!"

Our families need that active love that transforms and elicits love from others.

In his letter to the Corinthians, after St. Paul speaks of kindness, he introduces several negatives, I suppose because it is often easier to comprehend an idea that is expressed in the negative.

Love is not jealous, he says. Although some translations use the word "envy," most likely "jealous" is the preferred word. Lewis Smedes, the articulate author and professor at Fuller Theological Seminary, wrote that jealousy and envy are not the same. When we wish that we had something that belongs to someone else, we envy. The people we envy are not a threat to us and there is little pain in envy. Jealousy, on the other hand, is directed toward someone who threatens us and there is pain in jealousy. A daughter might envy her mother's knowledge about cooking but feels no pain about it, but that daughter will feel jealousy when her sister's mousse is praised and her own mousse turns out badly. Jealousy occurs when someone gets what we have or what we think we deserve and, therefore, we are threatened.

In families the dread phenomenon called "sibling rivalry" is a form of jealousy. Families have spouse rivalry, too, when one partner is perceived to be more attractive or successful. People who are loved and have healthy self-esteem do not usually suffer from jealousy or envy. They are quick, in fact, to rejoice at the good fortune of others. Love is not conceited or proud or ill-mannered. Lewis Smedes says love has "poise." Referring to the Revised Standard Version's translation, *Love is not boastful or arrogant or rude,* he provides a new insight:

> Boasting is a way of trying to look good when we suspect we are not good. Arrogance is an anxious grasp for power when we fear that we are weak. Rudeness is putting people down in order to try to hold ourselves up. All three result from a loss of balance that comes when we are empty at the center. Love is the power of poise because it provides balance at the center of our lives.[12]

When we are aware of God's love for us and have a healthy self-esteem, we feel no need to make ourselves look good by puffing ourselves up or by making others look bad.

Love is not selfish or, as the Revised Standard Version puts it, *Love does not insist on its own way.* Families are in trouble when one or more members always insist on their own way. To be sure, there are appropriate occasions for standing for personal rights, but there is no place in a healthy family for the selfish spirit that wants the others in the family always to revolve around one's own self. In healthy families the members are more concerned about giving than getting and, at the least, are willing to compromise and to give and take.

In the same sentence that Paul admonishes us about selfishness, he adds that "Love is not irritable." Irritability is an attitude or disposition that indicates a loveless spirit and is a form of selfishness. Though difficult, it can be conquered when we experience the love of God in Jesus.

Love does not keep a record of wrongs. Relationships are eroded when a family member recalls all the times he has been wronged and conveniently brings them up weeks, months, even years later! Love has a short memory of wrongs and injustices. Love forgives and puts things in the past and leaves them there.

Love is not happy with evil but is happy with the truth. Love does not gloat over others' misfortunes but rejoices when good things come to other people.

And best of all, love never gives up. Love keeps on loving when others have long ago given up. Over the years I have seen amazing long-suffering love from families for a member with a drinking problem or an emotional or physical illness or a long siege of rebellion and occasionally even a long case of infidelity. Sometimes there are wonderful victories to celebrate.

If I substitute in the passage from First Corinthians the word "Jesus" for the word "love" I get a good, clear

picture of his response to the circumstances of his life
and to us, as well:

Jesus is patient and kind; Jesus is not jealous
or conceited or proud; Jesus is not ill-mannered or
selfish or irritable; Jesus does not keep a record of
wrongs; Jesus is not happy with evil, but is happy
with the truth; Jesus never gives up; and his faith,
hope and patience never fail.

5

Being There
for Someone Else

Life is difficult.
This is a great truth, one of the greatest truths.[13]
— M. Scott Peck, M.D.

Help carry one another's burdens,
and in this way you will obey the law of Christ.
Galatians 6:2,3

Scott Peck begins his phenomenal best-seller *The Road Less Traveled* with the simple but profound statement, "Life is difficult." I readily agree!

Life *is* difficult! It is difficult to keep our personal lives on an even keel. It is difficult to keep the family going. It is difficult to keep things at work or school running smoothly. We all carry rather heavy loads as we struggle through life.

We do not all carry the same loads, however, and some burdens are heavier than others. Some burdens are thrust upon us that are not of our own making. We have no choice in the selection of our ancestors who may transmit physical or mental handicaps that have been passed on to them by their parents and others in their line. Some people contend all their lives with economic deprivation or with racial discrimination. Others are carrying heavy burdens because of injuries suffered in accidents or because they are victims of crippling and perhaps deadly disease.

Yet all of us carry burdens that are of our own making, as well. In some cases, we decide on a course of action that we know is right but that will carry with it a burden of hardship — perhaps loss of job or support of family and friends. In other cases, we make foolish judgments and have to pay a dear price. Even worse, sometimes we actively pursue an evil or immoral course of action, which then means that we are loaded down with a heavy burden of guilt, punishment, and loss of respect.

Some burdens that we carry actually belong to other people. Here I am thinking of heartache and concern that we feel for loved ones and friends. In some cases for parents with a wayward, struggling, or ill child. In some cases for children with wayward, struggling, ill or aging parents. In some cases for a husband or wife with a wayward, handicapped, or ill spouse. Most of us hurt when our loved ones and friends hurt.

Burdens are more easily carried with the help and love and support of others. However, there are always a few rugged individualists who doggedly resist any help from others and who offer no help to others. In one sense I admire their independent and tenacious spirit, but I also feel sorry for them because burdens are lighter when they are shared, and some of life's greatest joys come in helping others carry their loads. Those persons are depriving themselves of both help and the joy of giving. Most of us, though, can use all the help we can get! Most of us appreciate the help and love and support we receive from others, and most of us relish the satisfaction that comes from helping others.

It is not surprising, therefore, that the Apostle Paul, in his letter to the Galatians, appealed to his readers, *Help carry one another's burdens, and in this way you will obey the law of Christ.* Jesus was known as the man for others. It was his nature and his way to reach out in love and service. Paul indicates in this scripture that we follow Jesus' example and act in his spirit when we reach out in practical helpfulness to others to ease their burdens.

How can we help others carry their burdens?

For one thing, *we can support each other in prayer.* I cannot explain scientifically how it works, and I cannot

55

prove that prayer changes things, but I know from personal experience and from the testimony of others that the prayerful support of others can be very helpful in making burdens lighter — if for no other reason than that we are extremely encouraged as we become aware that others care and are concerned. I personally believe — even if I cannot prove it — that through prayer, spiritual forces of healing and strength are released and utilized. I do not believe that when God hears prayerful petitions coming to him from all directions he is *convinced* to help. I believe that through prayer his constant love is channeled to the person who is the object of the prayer.

Praying for others enhances our own spiritual growth, as well, and increases our concern. On some occasions, it even opens up practical ways by which we can practically and better serve the needs of the person about whom we are concerned.

We can help in another way by the ministry of listening. Indeed, I am quite convinced that listening to others is the single most helpful thing that we can do. Often when we are called in to be caregivers, we worry about what we will say. I understand and feel that anxiety myself, but in reality listening is more important than speaking. It is no accident that God made us with two ears and just one mouth! In most situations we should do at least twice as much listening as talking. The important thing is to be there and to try to meet other persons where they are. Many, many people are in desperate need for someone to listen to them.

To listen to someone, really listen, is to take that person seriously. To listen halfheartedly, or with the mind on one's own response, is to reveal more concern for self than for the other person. In one segment of the cartoon *The Family Circus*, little Jeffy is looking up at his father, who is sitting in his chair reading the newspaper. Jeffy says, "You hafta listen to me with your eyes, Daddy. Not just your ears." Jeffy was right. His father was more interested in the paper than he was in listening to Jeffy, and he was not taking the child seriously, adding to Jeffy's burden instead of helping him carry it.

Besides prayer and a listening presence, we need to offer practical helpfulness. To tell someone "Call me if you need me" is not enough. Far more effective is to take a meal over or baby-sit or transport kids or run errands.

We also ease others' burdens by simple courtesy. Sylvia and I were traveling recently and quite by accident learned that the warm and smiling waitress who welcomed us into a North Carolina restaurant had a heavy burden. An overheard conversation revealed that her fourteen-year-old son had received all the radiation and chemo he could tolerate and probably would not be able to return to school again. We heard her say, "He's trying so hard to be a man about it, and it just breaks my heart."

Later, in the car, Sylvia and I agreed that we never know what burdens people are carrying. Sometimes we are impatient and unreasonable in our demands or impolite with people we encounter casually, especially if we are waiting for service. If we could somehow be sensitive to the fact that a lot of people are carrying loads unknown to us, we would make extra effort to make their loads lighter simply by being patient.

In the Apostle Paul's letter to the Galatians (6:5), after urging them (us) to help each other carry life's burdens, Paul seems to contradict himself when he says that *"everyone has to carry his own load."* But this contradiction is only apparent, for the "load" he refers to is responsibility. The fact is that we cannot and should not try to relieve people of their responsibilities. As much as a man would like to, he cannot make his new bride happy. Her happiness must come from inside herself! As much as a father would like to, he cannot make decisions for his children in their recently achieved adulthood! No matter how much a mother hurts when she sees them making decisions that she feels are the worst decisions they could possibly make, their decisions are their responsibility.

As Peck says, "Life is difficult. This a great truth, one of the greatest truths." The loads we carry come in all weights and sizes. We cannot assume others' responsibilities for them, but we can listen. We can give practical help. We can be there for them. We can make life less difficult. This is another of the "greatest truths"!

6

Getting It All Together

I'm not saying that I have this all together, that I have it made. But I am well on my way, reaching out for Christ, who has so wondrously reached out for me. Friends, don't get me wrong: By no means do I count myself an expert in all of this, but I've got my eye on the goal, where God is beckoning us onward — to Jesus. I'm off and running, and I'm not turning back.

So let's keep focused on that goal, those of us who want everything God has for us. If any of you have something else in mind, something less than total commitment, God will clear your blurred vision — you'll see it yet! Now that we're on the right track, let's stay on it.

Philippians 3:12-16 (TM)

The word "focus" is normally used in the context of vision; that is, clearing up blurred vision with the lens of a camera or with glasses. Athletic coaches use it, though, to mean concentration and commitment. The first time I heard the word "focus" used in athletics was in a statement by Bill Curry when he was the head football coach at the University of Alabama. Bill Curry meant that he was trying to keep his team from being distracted by trivial concerns or by a tough opponent coming up later on the schedule. He wanted the team to concentrate on the task at hand. He wanted each player to get his priorities straight.

The most successful businesses, industries and institutions emphasize focusing; that is, a clear set of goals toward which they work and the elimination of distractions. Without worthy goals we flounder aimlessly, but with a point of focus we become productive. Good athletic teams set worthy goals for their season.

Individuals need to do the same. *USA Weekend* once carried a story from the early days of Lou Holtz, now the highly successful football coach at Notre Dame. Holtz said that when he was twenty-eight years old and an assistant coach at South Carolina, he invested heavily in a new home. His wife was eight months pregnant when the university's head coach suddenly left to take another job and Holtz found himself unemployed and going nowhere.

His wife bought him *The Magic of Thinking Big*, in which David Swartz says that we should write down all the goals that we want to achieve before we die. Holtz compiled a list of 107 goals and found himself excited about the possibilities in his life. "My whole life changed," he said. His life changed, in effect, because setting goals led him to a new philosophy and new attitudes.

Years later, after Notre Dame lost to Texas A&M in the Cotton Bowl, Holtz called a team meeting and talked to the players about being perfect in the classroom, on the field, and in personal character. Then he asked for everyone who wanted to win the national championship to stand up. Everyone stood up. That winter he initiated early morning workouts. When the players began to grumble and complain, Holtz would remind them: "You remember, you're the guys who stood up and said you wanted to be great." In the long run, the agreed-upon goal and the rugged discipline of practice paid off. The next year they were national champions.

Christians are called to be focused people. Too many of us have been content simply to be names on a church roll, exposing ourselves occasionally to the Spirit and Jesus in worship and church school but without any goals for growth in the Christian life and experience. Consequently, our Christian faith does not mean very much to us and in difficult times does not provide us with the kind of resources we need.

Stephen Covey, in *The Seven Habits of Highly Effective People*, writes about two different kinds of focus in different people. Proactive people, he says, focus their efforts on the things they can do something about. The nature of their energy is positive, enlarging and magnifying. Reactive people focus their efforts on the weakness of other people and circumstances over which they have no control. The nature of their energy is negative. Their focus results in blaming and accusing attitudes, reactive language, and increased feelings of victimization.[14]

We could learn a great deal about positive focus from the great Apostle Paul, who was certainly a focused Christian. Writing to the people at Philippi (Philippians 3:12-14), he spoke of his lifetime goal of being like Jesus Christ:

> *I do not claim that I have already succeeded or have already become perfect. I keep going on to try to win the prize for which Christ Jesus has already won me to himself. Of course, brothers, I really do not think that I have already won it; the one thing I do, however, is to forget what is behind me and do my best to reach what is ahead. So I run straight toward the goal*

in order to win the prize, which is God's call through Christ Jesus to the life above.

Paul is not known for his humility, but here he acknowledges that he is far from reaching his goal of Christlike qualities. He does, however, know where he wants to go and how he expects to get there. The phrase, *The one thing I do,* indicates to me that he is entirely focused. If only I could narrow my scope in that way! Most of us have let our lives become cluttered with too many distractions — not all bad, mind you, but often trivial and unnecessary. Most of us, in fact, could stand a little purging, so that we can focus on that which is most important and fulfilling. We have to decide what our highest priorities are. We have to have the courage to say "no" to the good in order to focus on the best.

"The one thing I do," Paul says, *"is to forget what is behind me."* With every year of life we accumulate a lot of emotional baggage that we carry around with us. Some of it is good. A lot of it we would be better off without. It weighs us down and prevents us from being our best.

To focus on the task at hand and pursue our goals we have to leave the past in the past. Certainly we should learn from past experiences so that we will not repeat past mistakes and can improve on past successes, but I think he is writing here not so much about learning from history as letting what has happened in the past control our present and future.

Surely he means that we should not rest on past laurels. To achieve worthy attainments is good and we are entitled to enjoy the recognition, but there comes a time when we have to let go and move on to other accomplishments. A star athlete in high school won't be remembered long for his accomplishments there. He becomes a pitiful figure if his claim to fame continues to be based on old glories.

To forget what is behind me means also we should not wallow in past guilt. Not to be released from past sins and mistakes can be a terrible burden to carry in the present and the future. I often experience this feeling when playing golf! Sometimes I will shoot a horrendously huge score on one of the early holes in a round and my tendency is to get angry and discouraged and to think that the rest of the round is ruined. If I do not put it out of my mind, I will shoot a terrible round. Many times, however, when I have been able to put that bad hole behind me, I have been able to finish with a respectable score after all.

Having put past accomplishments and mistakes behind him, Paul then says that he is able to press on toward his goal of Christlike faith and character. Paul uses strong words here that certainly describe focusing: *I do my best to reach what is ahead* and *I run straight toward the goal in order to win the prize.* He is so focused on his goal that he stretches every muscle and nerve to cross the finish line. The clear implication here is that to reach his goal he makes use of all the tried and true spiritual disciplines: prayer, worship, study of the scriptures, and service to humankind.

Like Paul, I am not saying that I have it all together. Like Paul, I would like to say that I'm well on my way, reaching out to Christ. Like Paul, I admit that I am not an expert in these matters. Unlike Paul, I'm not sure whether I have put the constraints of the past behind. I know, however, that I am committed to the practices of prayer, worship, study and service. I pray that my vision, like Paul's, remains clear so that I can keep my eye on the goal and maintain a total commitment as God beckons me onward — to Jesus Christ.

7

Becoming
What We Think

Man, I'm hammered, he thinks. He presses on deep into the night, so deep that he still is drinking when he notices the place is closed, the doors are locked and everybody else except the people who work in the club have gone home. That's when one of the employees pulls out the bag of cocaine. You want some?

I know I shouldn't, he thinks. But that notion passes quicker than one of his old fastballs, dissolving completely into the fuzziness of his alcohol-polluted mind. What the hell, he thinks, I'm on minor league rehab for my toe. They won't test me.

Within 48 hours a representative of the testing agency used by Major League Baseball arrives in Binghamton, N.Y., home of the Mets' Double A affiliate, to collect a urine sample from Dwight Gooden.[15]

Most of us have heard the old maxim: Sow a thought and you reap an act. Sow an act and you reap a habit. Sow a habit and you reap a character. Sow a character and you reap a destiny.

It became true for Dwight Gooden, who was National League Rookie of the Year and a millionaire before he was twenty-five years old and is today suspended from the game of baseball.

It's true of numerous doctors, lawyers, merchants, and chiefs. It is true of men and women wearing clergy collars and handsome clerical gowns. Several famous preachers in modern times, including Jim Bakker and Jimmy Swaggart and other Protestant clergy and some Catholic priests, have shown us how it works.

I am the product of my own thoughts. My "physical me" responds and reacts to the "mental me." My life — today, tomorrow, and as long as I live — is determined by what I think and the mental food that I put into my mind.

Norman Vincent Peale's book *The Power of Positive Thinking* promptly became a best-seller when it was published some years ago. It is still so widely read that Dr. Peale is immediately identified with the title and the theme of the book. His thesis is that a positive mental attitude can turn failure into success and defeat into victory. Some theologians, claiming to be realistic about the problem of evil in the world and the sinfulness of human beings, have denounced Dr. Peale and his theory. Nevertheless, the movers and shakers in business, industry, education, government, and the professions have been people who have practiced positive thinking and are clear proof of its power. It has been demonstrated in the laboratory of human experience, in all fields of endeavor, that those with positive mental attitudes will outperform negative-thinking competitors practically every time.

In sports the mental attitude will many times be the difference between winning or losing. I remember a time when Arkansas was to play in the Orange Bowl against Oklahoma, which was favored by twenty-three points. The Arkansas coach knew that his team lacked confidence in their ability to win the game, so he called a team meeting and asked each player to stand up, one by one, and say why he thought Arkansas could win. As they did, Coach Lou Holtz said he could see their whole attitude change. By game time confidence was on every Arkansas player's face, even though two outstanding starters on their team had been suspended for breaking training rules. Arkansas demolished Oklahoma that night.

Not only does our thinking make the difference between failure and success and between defeat and victory, but our thinking also shapes our basic character. The sage of Concord, Ralph Waldo Emerson, wisely said, "The thought is the ancestor of the deed." Leslie

Weatherhead, who preached in London for years, said "We become like the thoughts we think." The late Robert McCracken of New York's Riverside Church, in his sermon entitled "The Habitual Vision of Greatness" said essentially the same thing when he wrote, "How and what we think determines what we are."

David H. C. Read, former pastor of New York's Madison Avenue Presbyterian Church, made this insightful observation:

> The kind of person you are, and the kind of things you do, are very largely determined by the kind of images, or pictures, with which you fill your mind. We may think that we decide rationally what we want to be and do, but we are really much more influenced by the images on which we dwell. Suppose a girl wants to become a great ballet dancer. Her success will depend not so much on her willingness to work, her determination to pay the price of rigorous training and discipline, as on her constant mental picture of herself as a prima ballerina. In the most important question of all, the development of our Christian character, we are much more dependent on the images that fill our mind than on a series of rules for becoming a saint.[16]

Because St. Paul was very well aware of the sordid power of evil in the world, he knew the importance of

72

cultivating high and noble thinking. In his letter to the Philippians he pleaded with his readers:

> *In conclusion, my brothers, fill your minds with those things that are good and deserve praise: things that are true, noble, right, pure, lovely, and honorable. Put into practice what you learned and received from me, both from my words and from my deeds. And the God who gives us peace will be with you.*

Philippians 4:8-9

He did not simply say that we should *be* true, noble, right, pure, lovely and honorable. That would be like trying to follow a certain set of rules — better than nothing, perhaps, but totally inadequate. Instead, he urges us to *fill our minds,* to cultivate in our thinking the mental images of those noble qualities. This is a positive action each of us can take.

David Read expresses the idea well:

> And when we do [cultivate such images] we shall find that it is possible to switch our thoughts from the ugly, the sensual, the bitter, the anxious, to that which is good and happy and lovely and honorable. And when we do, our imaginings will nearly always soar toward those people in whom we have seen these qualities. Inevitably for the Christian the picture that will come most readily to our imagination will be that of our Lord himself.[17]

In this connection I have been greatly helped by an old and small book by James Allen called *As a Man Thinketh*. In it Allen likens the human mind to a garden:

Just as a gardener cultivates his plot, keeping it free from weeds, and growing the flowers and fruits which he requires, so may a person tend the garden of his mind, weeding out all the wrong, useless and impure thoughts, and cultivating toward perfection the flowers and fruits of right, useful, and pure thoughts. By pursuing this process, a person sooner or later discovers that he is the master gardener of his soul, the director of his life. He also reveals within himself the laws of thought and understands with ever-increasing accuracy how the thought-forces and mind-elements operate in the shaping of his character, circumstances and destiny.[18]

In today's world we are bombarded by sinister and diabolical messages that seek to control our thinking and, therefore, to shape our character and behavior. The most powerful of these come from television and the movies and, to a lesser degree, novels. Through those media we are constantly exposed to explicit and illicit sex, violence, lawlessness and filthy language. Even the "harmless" and "fun" cartoons that children watch are crammed full of violence. These harmful messages are so pervasive and so commonplace that most of us have become insensitive to them, and slowly but surely we have let our personal standards down.

Some years ago the Motion Picture Association of America eliminated the X category from its rating system and put in its place a new category NC-17. While X-rated movies were usually seen only in certain theaters in certain areas, with the new rating the violent and pornographic films that were formerly rated X now receive a wider and younger audience.

Our daughter Angela once came home from a movie that she thought Sylvia and I should see. When I questioned her about its rating, she said that she didn't know why it was rated R. It was quite humorous and we would really love it, she said. She wanted to see it again, so one afternoon we all went.

Only minutes into the movie, Sylvia and I began to notice the vulgarity of the language and wondered why Angela had not picked up on it. Afterwards, she was very embarrassed. "The language was gross!" she said. As we rode home and discussed the matter, we concluded that Angela hears that coarse language so much, at school and on television and at the movies, that she really did not notice it the first time she saw the movie.

Some months ago *Forbes* magazine interviewed Aleksandr Solzhenitsyn about politics and religion and business in Russia since the fall of communism. He was asked "Many Russians today are under the influence of

75

Western culture. Is that good?" He responded, "Russia is currently adopting many things from the West. Unfortunately, it is also adopting many of the worst things. All the filth! Pornography, drug addiction, organized crime, new types of swindles."[19] In the television documentary filmed as Solzhenitsyn traveled across Russia when he returned to that country after his lengthy stay in the United States, he often indicated that there has always been a curtain between the U.S. and Russia but that now "liquid manure" (meaning, of course, the pornography, drug addiction, and crime) was seeping under the curtain into Russia.

One of the major sources of friction between the U.S. and the Mideast nations is the immorality in our culture. It is not without reason that we are characterized by some Mideast leaders as "the great satan."

For ourselves and for the world that is looking to us for leadership we need to read good and wholesome books and articles, literature that enhances spiritual growth. We need to provide and encourage those same activities for our children and youth. We must find a way to curb the influence of the immorality which characterizes much television programming. We need to be serious and creative about Christian education.

We are in fact engaged in a war for minds, our own and those of our children and youth, and we dare not lose it! If the garden of the mind is not carefully cultivated by planting good seeds in it, bad seeds will fall into it. If they are not weeded out, they will produce their own kind. In our highly graphic media society, we are vulnerable to all kinds of harmful seeds being planted in our minds without realizing it. Slowly and surely our personal standards are crowded out, our values are eroded, our spirits tarnished by the corrosive acids of filth and vulgarity.

For this precise reason we must *fill our minds with those things that are good and that deserve praise: things that are true, noble, right, pure, lovely, and honorable.* St. Paul's promise to the Philippians holds true for us, as well. If we can follow his advice, the God who gives us peace will be with us.

77

8

Where Is God When I Suffer?

The questions of the night all blend into one. "Where is God when I suffer?" . . . It's the question of prolonged sickness, of unexplainable calamity, of life's bitter reversals. The inevitability of the questions of the night. We try with Kafka to "see through the thickness of things" and feel what Camus called "the hopeless encounter between human questioning and the silence of the universe." T. S. Eliot in his *Murder in the Cathedral* said that "Humankind cannot bear very much reality." But when the night of suffering comes with its stark reality, there is no alternative. And then we are faced with the ultimate temptation — to make God our adversary and not our advocate. We say with the psalmist, "Why has thou forgotten me?" That's the dark night of the soul.[20]

Lloyd Ogilvie poses the questions that sometimes come to us in the sleepless darkness of the early morning hours, and reflects the questions asked by Christians for a thousand years or more. Where is God when I suffer? Why does God allow suffering? Does he send it as a punishment? If so, what did I do to deserve this? Does God send trials, sickness, and problems into my life to discipline me? Must I accept this as the will of God?

Quite often tragedy is assumed to be God's will. We get angry at God for either causing it or allowing it to happen. The "why" questions and the anger at God are especially intense if I have been doing the best I can and it seems that God is singling me out to suffer without reason or if the person who is suffering is known to be a good person. If tragedy occurs to a person who is known to be of low moral character, we may be quick to say that it happened as divine punishment, but we have great difficulty reconciling our belief in a God of love with a tragedy that brings suffering to a person whom we know is good. These questions were asked frequently during the days following the bombing of the federal building in Oklahoma City.

The questions about God's role in these painful and puzzling situations hang heavily upon us. While I do not have all the answers to the role of God in human suffering, and I do not know anyone who does, I have struggled with these questions for over a quarter of a century and have some thoughts that are helpful to me. I hope they will be helpful to you.

Ironically, the Christian faith intensifies the problem and the mystery of human suffering. If there is no God or if there is a God like that of the Deists, remote and unconcerned about the world, then there is no reason why there shouldn't be widespread and indiscriminate suffering. But if there is a God of love, then for believers the mystery of suffering and the burden of explanation become very acute.

The unbeliever, on the other hand, has difficulty explaining the good in the world. How can he explain the life and work of Jesus Christ? Or the millions upon millions of others who are devout in their faith and generous, even self-sacrificing, in their service for others? Deep in the heart of every person is the need to love and to be loved and to live a noble contributing life. How is that need explained without a belief in a loving God?

The unbeliever's dilemma is peripheral to our discussion, however. At the heart of the believer's questioning are two widely held beliefs that I think should be rejected.

First, we must reject the belief that all suffering is due to sin, specifically some sin committed by the sufferer. This belief was widely held in Orthodox Judaism in Old Testament times. When Job was suffering, his friends tried to help him by urging him to recognize that he must have sinned grievously to be suffering so much. To Job's credit, he repeatedly

81

rejected their premise. But that belief continued into New Testament times. Jesus faced it on more than one occasion and flatly rejected it. To be sure, he would say that all sin leads to suffering, but he did not believe that all suffering was the direct result of some sin.

That belief is still with us, unfortunately. Often in the aftermath of a tragedy some people will castigate themselves and add unnecessarily to their grief, believing that God must be punishing them for some sin they have committed, perhaps something as trivial as missing Sunday School or Worship. Certainly we suffer because of our collective sinfulness, and sometimes, as when a person is hit by a drunk driver, we suffer because of the sinfulness of others. But one thing is sure: the God revealed in Jesus does not go about zapping us with tragedies to punish us for our sin. God did not cause the Oklahoma City bombing as an instrument of retribution.

We also need to reject the belief that all suffering comes from God. This belief is widespread and understandably so. After all, we reason, if God is God, and therefore the first cause of all things, then ultimately he is to blame for everything that happens. Even if we can't hold him to that axiom, if he is God and therefore is all-powerful, we think, he could certainly intervene and prevent tragedies to good people. Thus, we often ask strong questions:

Why did God do this to me?

Why did God let this happen?

Why didn't God do something to keep this from happening?

Is this God's will?

No human being can fathom the divine mysteries about God's will in life and death and suffering issues. I have been greatly helped over the years by Leslie Weatherhead's little book, now a classic, entitled *The Will of God.* I have been especially helped by his distinction between God's intentional will and his circumstantial will.[21]

God's *intentional will* is what God intends or wants to happen. God intends or wants us to be healthy, growing, active, fulfilled people. God does not intend or want us to be sick or injured or crippled. He does not want us to suffer from debilitating diseases or accidents, and God does not inflict such hardships or pain upon us.

I cringe when I hear people attribute suffering and pain to God and say that the suffering and pain are his will. I cringe when I hear people say that God must have caused them to suffer so that they could learn something from suffering or grow from it. I hope that they do learn something and I hope they grow from it, but I do not believe that God sends suffering to them for

83

that or any other reason. Some people, I know, find comfort in believing that their suffering is the will of God, but I can't. The God I see revealed in Jesus would never intentionally inflict suffering on anyone. If that God would, then Jesus and all others who engage in a ministry of healing and attempt to alleviate human suffering are attempting to thwart God's intentional will for human life!

God's circumstantial will is what God allows to happen within certain circumstances. God has made the universe orderly and has caused it to operate according to certain natural, immutable laws. He has also made human beings with free will, the capacity to choose. We would not have it otherwise. But those conditions also make suffering inevitable because human beings with free will make mistakes, will sin, and will run counter to divine laws, causing suffering and pain. Please think this through with me carefully. It is not God's intentional will that we do these things but God's circumstantial will. It is not God's intentional will that a person walk out into a busy street and be run over by a car, but it is God's circumstantial will that he allows such mishaps to happen. It is not God's intentional will that because of human or mechanical error a plane crashes, killing hundreds of people, but it is God's circumstantial will that he will allow this sort of thing to happen. God is not going to protect mechanics or pilots from errors, and he is not going to suspend the natural law of gravity.

We sometimes think that the world would be wonderful if God had made it so that there would be no possibility of accidents or disease or pain or suffering of any kind, but in actuality that kind of world would be terrible. The laws of nature would have to be extremely flexible. Sometimes an object would have to be hard and solid and sharp and at other times it would have to be soft and dull. There would be no need to work. There would never be an occasion to be concerned for others. There would be no sense of urgency to do anything. To be sure, there would never be any wrong actions, but there would be no place for courage or fortitude or generosity or kindness or prudence or unselfishness. If we want the assets of God's orderly and law-abiding and challenging world, then we have to accept also its liabilities. Being able to separate in my mind God's intentional will (or what he wants) from his circum-stantial will (or what he allows) I can understand why Christians and all good people are susceptible to all the diseases and accidents and other tragedies that come to all people.

Though this distinction is helpful to me, there is still a lot of mystery here. A lot of questions are unanswered, and probably we will not have answers until we meet God in the next life. But the good news of our faith is that even if God does not offer us an explanation for our suffering and even if he does not intervene to protect good people from suffering, he does offer us his presence in our suffering and the promise of victory over our suffering.

In Jesus, God came to be one of us, experiencing our human life in its fullness, including terrible suffering. Though he was a good man — indeed, a perfect man — Jesus experienced suffering all his life: poverty, rejection, oppressive political tyranny, even death itself. His death was not a peaceful dying in his sleep but a long, excruciatingly painful, humiliating death by crucifixion on a cross, where, by the way, he asked his own "why" question when he cried out, "*My God, my God, why have you forsaken me?*" He can therefore empathize with us in all our suffering. He knows how and what we feel. And so, when we are in the midst of terrible suffering, we can know that our God is standing beside us, loving us and understanding exactly what we are going through. St. Paul, in a powerful passage in Romans 8:28-39, assures us of this fact.

I cannot spell out how each person can experience that victory over suffering. Nor can I spell out what St. Paul meant when he said, "*We know that in all things God works for good with those who love him.*" He did not say, although the older translations of the Bible put it this way, that "all things work together for good." That translation is false and poor. Things do not always work for good for us, but it is true that "*in all things God works for good.*" This truth must have been hard for those who lost loved ones in Oklahoma City to grasp. This truth is hard to appreciate when we are close to the tragedy or the illness, but as time goes by and we get further removed from the tragic event, hopefully we grow in depth of character. We learn to appreciate more the love and support of others and the preciousness of time.

We will probably never have an adequate explanation for the mystery of human suffering in this life, but the good news of our Christian faith is that in Jesus, God came to be with us in our suffering. Not only that, but he helps us to come through to victory. Remember that the agony and defeat of Good Friday turned into the victory over death in the Resurrection. The Resurrection victory of Easter means that he and, therefore, we — not evil and death — have the last word.

87

9

Accepting Forgiveness From God

In the movie *The Godfather* is a scene which is not in the book by Mario Puzo on which the movie was based. After the death of his aged father, who was known as "The Godfather" (played by Marlon Brando), Michael Corleone (Al Pacino) participates in this memorable scene as godfather in the baptism of his sister's child. The event occurs at the same time that Michael's gunmen, on his direct order, are murdering the heads of other families in the Mafia.

Michael, standing beside the baptismal font in a lovely Roman Catholic church, responds to the ritual from the priest who is performing the rite of baptism. Bloody and violent scenes of the actual killings are interspersed in vivid counterpoint with the beautiful and holy scenes of the baptism:

Priest: *Michael, do you believe in God, the Father Almighty, Creator of the heavens and the earth?*

Michael: *I do.*

Priest: *Michael, do you believe in Jesus Christ, his only son, our Lord?*

Michael: *I do.*

Priest: *Do you believe in the Holy Ghost, the Holy Catholic Church?*

Michael: *I do.*

The volume of the pipe organ, which has been playing quietly, swells into a violence of its own as the violence on the screen escalates.

Priest: *Do you renounce Satan and all the spiritual forces of wickedness that rebel against God?*

Michael: *I do renounce them.*

The noise of shooting subsides; the gang lords are dead amid the gore. The cacophonous organ reverts to lovely, quiet sacred music.

Priest: *Go in peace, and may the Lord be with you.*

While I have a strong feeling that everyone, with the possible exception of incredible sociopaths like Michael Corleone, deals with the problem of sin and guilt, surely most of us are honest enough with ourselves to acknowledge that we are sinful. And most of us struggle with how to handle this knowledge and the resulting guilt. I have to assume that we, unlike Michael Corleone, recognize that our sinfulness separates us from God and that we want to experience God's forgiveness of our sin. Jesus' parable of the prodigal son in Luke 15 can help us in getting at the experience of how God forgives us.

There was once a man, Jesus said, who had two sons. One day the younger son came to him and said, "Father, give me my share of the property now." Even without understanding the inheritance customs of that part of the world in that day, we can see arrogance in that request. The son was not polite or respectful. He was not willing to wait for his father's death to inherit his portion of the estate. He wanted it right then.

When the father granted his request, the son converted his holdings into cash and went to a country far away, thus embellishing his arrogance by adding hostility.

Out in the far country he wasted his money in reckless living and spent everything he had. At the same time in that country there was a famine — in our time, a deep recession or depression. He was, however, fortunate enough to be able to find work, though it was taking care of a man's pigs. How desperate he must have been! For a young Jewish man to be forced to take care of pigs was the ultimate insult to himself. Jesus makes

91

the son seem even more desperate with these words: "*He wished he could fill himself with the bean pods the pigs ate, but no one gave him anything to eat.*"

In these events we can discern the mechanics of human sinfulness. In the first place, the young man made a choice. For whatever reasons, he made the decision to demand his inheritance and to leave home. He was not forced out of the house and out of relationship with his father.

We sin and do wrong by our own choice. To be sure, there are genetic and environmental influences at work in our decisions. But, except in those cases of severe mental illness in which we are incapable of knowing the difference between right and wrong and are motivated by disturbed, warped thinking, we choose our actions and must bear responsibility for them.

The young man made the choice to be "free" and to live it up. He then made choices about use of his money that resulted in having to take the only job he could find, one that was personally degrading to him.

I have never known anyone who stood at the marriage altar with the intention in mind to get a divorce. I have never known anyone who was sitting quietly to enjoy a few drinks or some other kind of drugs who was planning to become an addict. I have never known anyone who swiped five dollars from his mother's purse who intended to become a criminal and end up in prison.

In all these cases, somewhere along the line some misguided or bad choices were made. Often we fail to listen to the good advice or experience of others who try to steer us in a different direction. Often we fail to listen to the inner voice which warns us of a wrong first step. Often we demonstrate a basic arrogance that demands independence from God and others.

Sin is the deliberate decision to rebel against God. It is a personal declaration of independence from God. It is deciding that we can handle our affairs better than God can. When this decision is made, we come under the power of sin and evil. We are not nearly as free as we think we are.

In his letter to the Romans the Apostle Paul very graphically describes what I call the "human predicament" in these words:

> *I do not understand what I do; for I don't do what I would like to do, but instead I do what I hate. . . . For even though the desire to do good is in me, I am not able to do it. I don't do the good I want to do; instead, I do the evil that I do not want to do. If I do what I don't want to do, this means that no longer am I the one who does it; instead, it is the sin that lives in me . . . . My inner being delights in the law of God. But I see a different law at work in my body — a law that fights against the law that my mind approves of. It makes me a prisoner to the law*

of sin which is at work in my body. What an unhappy man I am! Who will rescue me from this body that is taking me to death?

Romans 7:15-24

I can see myself all through these words! A generation ago Harry Emerson Fosdick wrote about this passage: "A truer description of a universal human problem it would be hard to imagine. The great seers have consistently said the same, from Plato describing the problem as driving a chariot with two horses, one white and eager, the other dark and obstinate, to Goethe's Faust, saying, 'Two souls, alas, are lodg'd within my breast.'"[22]

There are often times when I do not understand my actions, times when I know what is right and want to do what is right and will do the very thing I did not want to do. Like Paul, I find that I am often in a civil war in my own being, torn between what I know to be right and my desire to do right on the one hand and my inability to do right on the other hand. To some extent we are all in the far country, captive to the sin that reigns within us.

Granted, then, that we are sinners and truly sin, what do we do about it? Many of our attempts to deal with our sin are, alas, destructive.

One person tries to deny guilt and repress it.

Another tries to minimize sinfulness by comparing himself to other "worse" sinners.

94

Still another person tries to cover up sinfulness with drugs and alcohol.

All of these approaches are evasive and prove often to give only temporary, inadequate relief. The only adequate, permanent solution to the problem of sin and guilt is to receive the forgiveness of God. I say that because sin, even against other human beings, is basically sin against God. We were made in God's likeness. We were made to live our lives in a relationship of love with him. When we harm others, we actually sin against the objects of God's love. It follows, then, that only God can cure our sinfulness. His remedy is his forgiveness. Our healing begins as we accept his forgiveness.

While the rebellious son was away, the father always loved, hoping day after day that the son would return. Meanwhile, the son, in his desperate condition, came to his senses. He began to make plans to return, in a spirit of contrition and repentance and humility, and ask to be received, not as a son but as a hired servant.

When he neared home, before he could confess his sin and show repentance, his father saw him and ran to meet him, kissing him and welcoming him. His father did not utter any word of forgiveness. In his eagerness he did not even permit his son to complete his carefully rehearsed speech. When the son made his confession,

> . . . *the father wasn't listening. He was calling to the servants, "Quick. Bring a clean set of clothes*

95

and dress him. Put the family ring on his finger and sandals on his feet. Then get a grain-fed heifer and roast it. We're going to feast! We're going to have a wonderful time! My son is here — given up for dead and now alive! Given up for lost and now found!" And they began to have a wonderful time.

Luke 15:22-24 (TM)

The son had always been forgiven in his father's mind, for the father was that kind of person. Yet, the forgiveness could not be experienced, or become operative, until the son returned in repentance and humility. Although we must bear the consequences of our wrong-doing, confession and repentance are not conditions that we must meet to get God to forgive us.

The good news is that the free gift of God's forgiveness is extended to us for all of our sins before we confess or repent or perform any acts of restitution. The good news of the Gospel is that there is nothing that we can do to earn God's forgiveness or to motivate God to forgive us. He forgives us because he loves us and wants to forgive us. Like the loving father of the prodigal son, our Father welcomes us back to a loving relationship as if we have never been away.

10

Forgiving
Ourselves

But unfortunately, second times around don't happen. We cannot re-rear our children. I cannot re-live my first job. Initial impressions cannot be remade. Cutting remarks cannot be re-said. Scars can't be completely removed. Tear stains on the delicate fabric of our emotions are, more often than not, permanent. Memories are fixed, not flexible.

"You mean God won't forgive?"

"You know better than that."

"And people can't overlook my failures?"

"Come on, now. That's not the issue at all. Most people I know are amazingly understanding. Our biggest task is forgiving ourselves."[23]

God's act of restoring us to a relationship of love with him, as if we have never been away, should be good and welcome news to us. But, alas, as Chuck Swindoll writes, many of us have difficulty accepting God's forgiveness — perhaps because we are too oriented to our daily-world routine of justice and fair play. We feel that there must be something that we need to do to justify or to earn God's forgiveness. The good news of the Christian gospel is that God's forgiveness is a free gift, but the bad news is that persons often can't bring themselves to accept it.

A good first step toward acceptance is an honest confession of wrong-doing. Obviously the person who does not acknowledge his wrongdoing and need of forgiveness is not going to be receptive to God's forgiveness. Jesus himself said on one occasion that "You will know the truth and the truth will make you free." Whenever we face up to and acknowledge the truth about ourselves, we become free. The very basis of the phenomenal success of Alcoholics Anonymous in leading people to sobriety is an individual's admission of the need for help. As long as a person who is addicted to or has a problem with alcohol denies the problem, that person is living in a world of illusion and cannot be helped. Only with acknowledgement comes freedom to overcome the addiction.

All of us need, from time to time, to do personal moral self-inventory. Certainly, we need to confess to God, but it can also be helpful to talk out wrong-doings with a trusted friend or counselor or spiritual director.

Dietrich Bonhoeffer points out that sin withdraws us from community because sin wants to remain unknown.

"The more isolated a person is," he writes, "the more destructive will be the power of sin over him, and the more deeply he becomes involved in it, the more disastrous is his isolation."

When confession is made to God and to someone else, sin loses its power because it has been exposed and chased away by forgiveness. Bonhoeffer says,

> The expressed, acknowledged sin has lost all its power. It has been revealed and judged as sin. It can no longer tear the fellowship asunder. Now the fellowship bears the sin of the brother. He is no longer alone with his evil for he has cast off his sin in confession and handed it over to God. It has been taken away from him. Now he stands in the fellowship of sinners who live by the grace of God in the cross of Jesus Christ. Now he can be a sinner and still enjoy the grace of God. He can confess his sins and in this very act find fellowship for the first time.[24]

Cecil Osborne, in *You're in Charge,* tells about a young minister's wife, riddled with anxiety stemming from unresolved guilt. Dr. Osborne said that hers was largely false guilt, based on generalized feelings of inadequacy, rejection in childhood, and inability to feel acceptable to God, herself, or her husband. All of these emotions register on the unconscious mind as guilt. One evening at her weekly Yokefellow group meeting, she said, "I've just decided to join the human race and admit that I'm a sinner, and so what! Isn't that what it's all about — to admit it, confess it, and let God forgive us?"[25] The young woman had attended church and Sunday School all of her life, but only when she discovered acceptance in a loving group was she able to confess.

Closely tied to the act of confession is the act of repentance. Repentance is more than remorse, which is simply feeling sorry and regretful. A person can feel remorse for sin while continuing it. I know persons who are involved in wrongdoing — say, an extramarital affair — who suffer terrible guilt feelings and are remorseful but are unwilling to break away from the relationship. Of course, they have no freedom from guilt until they repent. Repentance is actually changing directions. It is turning from one loyalty to another. Repentance is actually turning away from sin. It is turning from sin to God.

Whenever possible, reasonable, and appropriate, it is incumbent upon us to make amends for our wrongdoing. We must remember, however, that we make restitution, not to get God to forgive us but to clear the channel by which we can be receptive to forgiveness.

I heard about an interesting letter that was received by the Internal Revenue Service:

Last year when I filed my income tax return I deliberately misrepresented my income. Now I cannot sleep. Enclosed is a check for $150 for taxes owed. If I still cannot sleep, I will send you the rest.

In a humorous way that letter shows the futility of simple remorse and of the need to make full restitution whenever it is possible, reasonable, and appropriate.

Sometimes restitution is not possible. We cannot, for example, make amends to someone who has died. Sometimes restitution may not be reasonable, when distance or other personal circumstances may be involved. Sometimes restitution is inappropriate, if innocent people could be hurt by an attempt to make restitution. In those cases we can only make our confession, do our own repentance, and trust in the grace, mercy and love of God to cover our wrongdoing.

If the feeling of forgiveness still eludes us, the problem is certainly within ourselves. Possibly we are afflicted with unrealistic perfectionism. To be sure, having high standards and goals for ourselves is commendable, but some of us find it practically impossible to believe that we are subject to the same weaknesses that are common to everyone else.

Alternately, the problem may be low self-esteem. Some persons have such little regard for themselves that they have difficulty believing that God would forgive them and, certainly, they cannot forgive themselves.

Lewis Smedes has pointed out that self-esteem and self-forgiveness are not the same. A healing response to our feeling of unworthiness is to understand that we are neither inferior nor superior. The truth is, I am simply me, and you are simply you. Self-esteem comes from realizing that we are made in God's likeness and are the object of his love. Smedes says, "You esteem yourself when you discover your own excellence. You forgive yourself after you discover your own faults. You esteem yourself for the good person you are. You forgive yourself for the bad things you did."[26]

Either unrealistic perfectionism or extremely low self-esteem is reason enough to seek the services of a good professional or pastoral counselor.

Whatever the reason, inability to forgive self may have actual physical consequences. Jesus was well ahead of his time in understanding that guilt and conflict can be debilitating. He was quite knowledgeable and perceptive about the relationships among body, mind, and spirit. Some of his miracles, for example, were not so much acts that defied natural laws as applications of his knowledge, wisdom, and love, that in fact cooperated with natural laws to bring about what seemed to be unexplainable results.

There are numerous documented cases of actual physical paralysis caused by mental guilt and spiritual conflict over wrongdoing. More common, though, are cases in which guilt-ridden persons cannot function in a normal, healthy way. We become fatigued easily. We cannot concentrate. Our resistance is lowered and we become susceptible to all kinds of illnesses. Some fall into despondency and depression.

Few of us recognize that the root of the problem is a sense of sin and the resulting guilt. Our efforts to cope with the problem deal only with the symptoms. The sad part is that the cure is simple and readily available: namely, hearing and accepting God's word of forgiveness.

Dr. Bill Wilson, an outstanding physician at the Department of Psychiatry at Duke University, is a very competent psychiatrist and a Christian. Bruce Larson tells of an incident involving one of Dr. Wilson's patients, a Vietnam veteran, who had been non-functioning for years. It was finally learned that, while performing his military duty in Vietnam, the man had been responsible for killing many people. When the medical staff was convinced that the man's mental illness was the result of his inability to forgive himself for what he had done, Dr. Wilson sat on the patient's bed and said, "I want to tell you that your sins are forgiven."

"What did you say?" the veteran asked incredulously.

"I have the authority to tell you that through Jesus Christ your sins are forgiven," Dr. Wilson repeated.

That exchange marked the beginning of the man's recovery. I am told that he resumed a place in society and functioned normally. In that case, Bruce Larson comments, Dr. Wilson was the instrument of a miracle of healing, not as a psychiatrist but as a Christian.

We Christians *know* intellectually that God forgives us, but sometimes we still feel guilty. Clearly then the problem is not with God but with ourselves. If "our biggest task is forgiving ourselves," we should remember what Paul wrote to the Christians in Rome:

> *What shall we say, then? That we should continue to live in sin so that God's grace will increase? Certainly not! We have died to sin — how then can we go on living in it? For surely you know this: when we were baptized into union with Christ Jesus, we were baptized into union with his death. By our baptism, then, we were buried with him and shared his death, in order that, just as Christ was raised from death by the glorious power of the Father, so also we might live a new life.*
>
> *For if we became one with him in dying as he did, in the same way we shall be one with him by being raised to life as he was. And we know this: our old being has been put to death with*

Christ on his cross, in order that the power of the sinful self might be destroyed, so that we should no longer be the slaves of sin. For when a person dies he is set free from the power of sin. If we have died with Christ, we believe that we will also live with him. For we know that Christ has been raised from death and will never die again — death has no more power over him. The death he died was death to sin, once and for all; and the life he now lives is life to God. In the same way you are to think of yourselves as dead to sin but alive to God in union with Christ Jesus.

Romans 6:1-11

To accept God's forgiveness but not to forgive yourself is self-righteous religious snobbery, isn't it? If you are having difficulty forgiving yourself, ask yourself this question: If God forgives me as the Gospel claims he does and I believe that he does, then who am *I* not to forgive *myself?*

105

11

Forgiving
Others

Some years ago a fine nineteen-year-old man in the church where I serve was killed in a head-on collision. The driver of the other car was a young Navy man who had had too much to drink. Not long after the funeral, the mother of the deceased called me to say that she wanted to go out to the Navy Hospital to visit the young man who had killed her son and asked me if I would arrange the visit and go with her. The Navy physician I called (who was a member of the church) to ask about the possibility of our visit told me that when the young man was physically and mentally able for the visit, he would let me know, so in a couple of weeks the mother, another church member and I drove out to the Navy Hospital. As we entered, I was somewhat tense, but I will never forget seeing that grief-stricken but brave mother take that young man's hand and tell him that she forgave him for what he had done. It was a hallowed moment. I do not know what legal and personal consequences he had to suffer later, but I do know that that mother, by that act, cleansed her system of any poisonous hate and resentment and, released from that burden, was able to put her life back together again.

While we welcome and rejoice over God's forgiveness, we sometimes recoil in horror over the need to forgive others. In fact, at times we would rather do almost anything and suffer almost any pain than forgive some persons for the way they have offended or mistreated or hurt us. Perhaps a spouse or family member or trusted friend who has been abusive. Perhaps an unfaithful spouse or a disloyal business partner who has caused us great pain. Perhaps a vindictive employer who has refused promotion or caused loss of job. Perhaps a stranger whose crime or carelessness has caused death or injury.

As a matter of fact, no matter how we look at it, to be asked to forgive some people seems to be unreasonable and unfair. After all, we live in a world that is based on justice and fair play and letting the punishment fit the crime. Logically, if you hurt me, then I should be allowed to hurt you equally, and I certainly should be able to justify continuing to resent you for what you have done to me. There is a delightful satisfaction in paying persons back for the wrong they have done to us. Revenge *is* sweet.

Although to forgive others is an extremely difficult thing to do, clearly in the New Testament the willingness to forgive others is a necessary condition for us to be able to receive God's forgiveness and, by implication, to forgive ourselves.

Simon Peter put a question to Jesus: "*Lord, if my brother keeps on sinning against me, how many times do I have to forgive him? Seven times?*" As difficult as it is to forgive someone once, Jewish law laid down that a person should extend forgiveness three times. Peter had been with Jesus enough to know that Jesus was very magnanimous and loving, so in his question Peter doubled the three and added one more! He must have thought that Jesus would be proud of him for *his* magnanimity!

Imagine then his surprise when Jesus answered, "*No, not seven times but seventy times seven.*" Clearly Jesus did not mean literally 490 times but unlimited and unending forgiveness.

A clear understanding of the forgiveness process requires an understanding of what forgiveness is not. Forgiveness is not forgetting. Oh, to be sure — in time, thank goodness — we can forget some things, but forgiveness is extending pardon for things that we often remember all too well.

109

Forgiveness is not excusing. As Lewis Smedes puts it, "We excuse people when we understand they were not to blame . . . we forgive people for things we blame them for."[27] I once received an extremely hateful letter which profoundly shook me. Not long afterwards, the writer of the letter was diagnosed as having a malignant brain tumor, so I assumed that he had written the letter when he was not really himself. I knew then that I could excuse him rather than forgive him. If my two-year-old, in his natural exploring, knocks a lamp off the table, I excuse him. If my son, when he was sixteen, had been caught driving under the influence of alcohol, I would have been called upon to forgive him.

Forgiveness is not condoning wrongdoing. It is restoring the personal relationship, often with the understanding that I do not approve the offending person's actions. Although the person might have to bear the consequences of the deed for some time, the deed is no longer an impediment to the relationship.

Similarly, forgiveness is not letting someone off the hook. When I have forgiven my sixteen-year-old for driving under the influence of alcohol and restored the relationship, he still needs to suffer the legal and other consequences of his wrongdoing.

Forgiveness does not always bring reconciliation. At least two parties are needed for a reconciliation. The offending party could be deceased or unwilling to reconcile. Two divorced persons might forgive each other but find it unwise or impractical to reconcile to the extent of renewing their marriage.

On a deeper level the simple but often unacknowledged fact is that the unwillingness to forgive does more harm to the person harboring resentment and the desire for revenge than it does to the offending person. Doris Donnelly, in her excellent book *Learning to Forgive*, lists ten probabilities that happen to people who are unwilling to forgive:

> They are led by their anger, pain, or hatred.
>
> They are directed by negative memories.
>
> They do not act freely.
>
> They keep a controlling grasp on situations and people.
>
> They are pressured by lives of tension and stress.
>
> They probably shorten their lives.
>
> Their relationships with others are strained.
>
> Their relationship with God is weakened.
>
> They live with feelings of little self-worth.
>
> They feel unrelieved guilt.[28]

When forgiving is difficult, we do well to remember that forgiving someone else is often first an act and then a feeling. If we wait until we feel pardon or good will toward the offender, we may be stuck, but if we initiate the first positive steps, then we can be sure that our feelings will in time change to positive ones also. A good place to begin is by first praying for God's help in forgiving the one who has offended and then praying for that person.

It helps to remember that we are all sinners and do wrong. To be sure, we might feel that someone has committed a more serious offense against us than we ourselves commit, and we might be right, but none of us can claim innocence or purity. In fact, we might have committed more serious sins of the spirit.

One of the main points in Jesus' parable of the unforgiving servant in Matthew 18:21-35 is that what God forgives us is very much, while what we forgive others is usually very little. Because of our own guilt, none of us has a right to sit in judgment or to condemn others.

> *There was once a king, he said, who had a servant who owed him millions of dollars.* [It was ludicrous, of course, to think that any servant could owe a king millions of dollars, and his listeners probably chuckled at that.] *The servant could not pay his debt, so the king ordered that the servant and his family be sold as slaves toward payment of the debt. The servant begged for mercy and promised to pay all his debts* [which would have been impossible]. *The king felt sorry for him and forgave him the debt and let him go.*

112

The servant immediately came upon a fellow servant who owed him a few dollars. The servant grabbed him and demanded that he pay his debts. The second servant begged for mercy and promised to pay his debt, but the first servant had the man thrown into prison until he could pay the debt.

When the king heard about it he immediately called the first servant in and said to him: "You worthless slave! I forgave you the whole amount you owed me, just because you asked me to. You should have had mercy on your fellow servant, just as I had mercy on you."

The king then had the man thrown into prison until he could pay back his debt. Jesus concluded the parable with these sobering words: *That is how my father in heaven will treat every one of you unless you forgive your brother from your heart.*

This is not an isolated teaching of Jesus. In his model prayer, which we call The Lord's Prayer, a prayer that we use regularly in public and private worship, we pray, *"Forgive us our debts as we forgive our debtors."* That phrase is the only petition in the prayer to which Jesus added emphasis: *If you forgive others the wrongs they have done to you, your father in heaven will also forgive you. But if you do not forgive others, then your father will not forgive the wrongs you have done.*

113

In spite of the direct, strong wording here, my sense of Jesus' meaning is not that God forgives us to the extent that we are willing to forgive others but that *if we are not willing to forgive others, we block the channel by which we are enabled to receive God's forgiveness.*

For many generations there has been a deep and bitter enmity between Armenia and Turkey. The great missionary E. Stanley Jones recorded the story about an Armenian nurse who with her brother was attacked by Turks. She escaped, but her brother was brutally killed before her eyes.

She was a nurse, and later on while nursing in the hospital recognized one of her patients as the very Turkish soldier who had murdered her brother. Her first feeling was: Revenge!

He was very ill, just hovering between life and death. The slightest neglect, and he would die. And no one would know. His life was absolutely in her hands. But instead of revenge she decided for Christ's sake to forgive him. She fought for his life and won, nursing him back to health.

When he was convalescent, she told him who she was. The Turkish soldier looked at her in astonishment and said, "Then why didn't you let me die, when you had me in your power?"

"I couldn't," answered the girl. "I just couldn't, for I am a Christian, and my own Master forgave His enemies who crucified Him. I must do the same, for His sake."

"Well," said the hardened Turk in astonishment, "If that is what it means to be a Christian, I want to be one."[29]

When we are willing to forgive, several good things are likely to happen. We often have the opportunity to renew a relationship with someone from whom we have been estranged. But more importantly, our minds and hearts and bodies are cleansed of the poison of hate and resentment. Also, we are rescued from an unpleasant past and freed to live in an open future. As a result, we are relieved of a lot of tension and stress. We are then able to attain and enjoy a new relationship with God.

12

Being "Born Again"

Charles M. Duke, Jr., was one of the two astronauts in Apollo-Saturn 16 who walked on the moon in the fifth lunar landing. After they collected 213 pounds of lunar samples and returned safely to earth, Astronaut Duke was asked if he had had a spiritual experience when he walked on the moon. He said that he had not, that he didn't think of God very much during the flight or when he got back from the moon and went to church every Sunday, as had been his custom even before the lunar flight.

When he learned that NASA wouldn't have anything much for him to do for about eight years while the space shuttle was perfected, he concentrated on making a lot of money. Once the goal of wealth was achieved, however, and his marriage began to fall apart, he no longer had the strong goal-orientation which had always fulfilled his life.

With financial security, his profession on hold and his marriage dissolving, he realized that something critical was missing. When he met God in Jesus Christ, Mr. Duke called this encounter being "born again."

How many of us at the pinnacle of our lives — not just astronauts, athletes, actors or entertainers — say, "Is this all there is?"

The need that Astronaut Duke sensed was the same need that drove Nicodemus, a leading Jew and Pharisee of Jesus' day. When Nicodemus approached him, Jesus introduced the powerful concept of being "born again." According to the Revised English Bible, the King James Version, and other translations, " . . . *no one can see the kingdom of God without being born again.*" It is a striking comment about the human condition, about the spiritual condition of mankind, and one to which we should pay careful attention.

Because this concept is so important, it is unfortunate that people today tend to divide followers of Jesus into two classifications: "conventional" Christians and "born-again" Christians. In that process this important concept is often denigrated.

"Conventional" Christians are usually found in the mainline denominations although some persons in these denominations consider themselves to be "born again."

In most cases the people in mainline denominations are people who have been reared in the Christian tradition. They've always known that Jesus loves them. They love him and seek to worship him regularly and to serve him as well as they can.

The "born-again" Christians tend to be most often found in the evangelical and charismatic churches. They, too, may have been reared in the Christian tradition, but most of them can point to some spiritual experience in which Jesus has become extremely real to them. Sometimes that experience is powerful and overwhelming. Sometimes it is a "charismatic" one. That is, the Holy Spirit of God overwhelms and empowers them. They can mark a decisive change in their lives from that experience that they say is like being born all over again.

While I personally rejoice whenever someone has that powerful life-changing experience of being "born again," I am saddened by an attitude that I often pick up from that group, a self-righteousness that tends to divide the church into first class Christians (the "born-again" types) and second class Christians (the "conventional" types). A generation ago the media would identify a person simply as a Christian. But now, the phrase "born-again Christian" is attached to certain persons who often display that fact with religious t-shirts and a lot of "God-talk." And, all the while, though we conventional types

119

do not especially want to be known as super pious or religious — or at least do not care to demonstrate our piety so openly — we do wonder why we have not had a powerful life-changing spiritual experience. Is there something wrong with us, we think, that the Holy Spirit has passed us by?

Making the concept more dramatic and worthy of our attention is Jesus' statement to Nicodemus in John's Gospel: *"I tell you the truth: no one can see the Kingdom of God unless he is born again."* That is a pretty strong statement! Jesus did not say that we should try to improve and be better people, that we should add new virtues and discard some bad habits. He said that we cannot see or enter the Kingdom of God unless we are born again.

What does this scripture mean to us conventional Protestant Christians? We must not simply disregard an important and wonderful concept simply because it has been preempted by conservative Christians. Certain aspects of Jesus' teaching must be closely examined if we are to realize fully the meaning of this provocative phrase.

We may be helped in this matter by looking closely at Jesus' encounter with Nicodemus. The Pharisee came to see Jesus presumably because he had a hunger to know about spiritual matters. Like Astronaut Duke, he must have realized that his life was not fully satisfying.

It blows my mind to imagine the scene when Jesus spoke to this successful, devout, morally straight leader in the church and the community: "Hey fellow, you're on the wrong track. You might think you're doing great, but you've got to do it all over differently. If you want to see or enter the Kingdom of God, you've got to make a new and radical change in your life that would be like being born all over again." If Nicodemus had been a hardened criminal or an immoral person, we could understand, but he was neither.

From this story in John 3:1-17 and other passages we know several important things about Nicodemus. First, he apparently was wealthy, for later we read that when Jesus died, Nicodemus bought for Jesus' body "one hundred pounds of spices, a mixture of myrrh and aloes." Only a wealthy man could buy such a quantity of burial ointments.

Also, we know that he was a Pharisee. Pharisees have a bad image in Christian circles because of their extreme legalism, but they could have been very good people. They committed themselves to observe every detail of the Jewish law. They had to study and know the law and then obey it, not an easy task at all. Across the centuries, the Scribes and others had tried to define the law by drawing up all kinds of definitions and regulations that made obeying the law extremely complex and difficult. Nicodemus was one of those elite people in the Jewish community who spent his life trying to obey all the laws and commandments.

From the phrasing in the various translations calling Nicodemus "Jewish leader" and "a Ruler of the Jews," we know that he was a member of the Sanhedrin, a court of seventy prominent people, considered the Supreme Court of the Jews. Even though the power of the Sanhedrin was somewhat limited under Roman rule, their powers were still extensive because the Romans permitted the Sanhedrin to have religious jurisdiction over the Jewish people. To be a member of that select group certainly suggests that Nicodemus was a man of leadership and prominence among his own people.

If we could transport Nicodemus into the twentieth century, he would probably be a highly successful professional person or executive type, most likely a CEO, an Episcopalian or Presbyterian, and a scrupulously religious man. We have no national equivalent to the Sanhedrin, but in our day Nicodemus would be an elder and he would likely be on the national board of his denomination and probably a member of the board of a seminary or some other church institution.

I am quite confident that Jesus was not in any way rejecting Nicodemus' accomplishments or putting him down personally. Indeed, most likely the scripture does not record everything that was said in this conversation. Clearly, however, Nicodemus did not understand what

Jesus meant by being born again and he took Jesus literally; that is, he thought Jesus meant a new physical birth. But Jesus meant a spiritual rebirth, a change of perception of who God is and who we are, a change in attitude, a change in lifestyle and orientation. Without that change, Jesus said, a person cannot see or enter the Kingdom of God.

We understand the Kingdom of God to be the rule or reign of God over the entire universe and over the affairs of nations. But the New Testament teaches further that in Jesus the Kingdom of God is very near to us. Jesus is the embodiment of the Kingdom of God. In his work and words we have a concrete example of how life is in the Kingdom of God.

In Jesus' works of healing, for example, we see God attacking illness and death. Consequently, when we work to defeat illness and death, we are doing the work of the Kingdom of God. In his teachings and in his personal relationships we see relationships in the Kingdom of God. Consequently, when we live in love with others and give to others, we are living the life of the Kingdom of God.

The key, however, is Jesus himself and how we perceive him and encounter him and relate to him. Whenever and however we come to see that he is the eternal Son of God, the Savior of the world, and the Lord of the universe, whenever we turn to him in faith so that

123

he becomes *our* Savior and *our* Lord, we are spiritually reborn and we see and enter the Kingdom of God.

The transformation can happen instantaneously in an overwhelming spiritual experience or it can happen gradually over a period of time. Nicodemus' problem was that he was trying to enter the Kingdom of God by his own accomplishments, by slavish obedience to laws and rules, and Jesus wanted him to see that God's Kingdom comes as a gift from God. Jesus invited Nicodemus to enter into a relationship of love with him which would be the beginning of a new life for him.

When we become aware of God's love for us, life becomes so different that it is like being born all over again. Some people, of course, do not believe in a God at all and they have to come up with their own basis for meaning in life and how to live it. Other people believe in a God so harsh and demanding and vindictive that they cower in fear. They might be good people, but their motive is to escape God's wrath. Some of us, though, have come to know the God who is revealed in Jesus Christ, and that God we know is one of love. He created us in love and reaches out to love us in many ways. He is willing to go to any lengths to let us know of his love for us, even a humiliating death on a cross in our behalf. Whenever and however we become aware of God's love for us — whether it be in a dramatic life-changing experience or whether it be a gradual realization, as in the case of most of us — life becomes radically different.

Left to our base instincts, we will grab and hoard for ourselves, trying to get others to love us, and will be disappointed to find that we are miserable. But having experienced God's love and forgiveness, we are then motivated to love and forgive others. As we reach out from ourselves and give to others, we begin to experience a deep joy in life that is radically different.

When we become aware of our assurance of life eternal because of Jesus' defeat of death in his Resurrection, life becomes so different that it is like being *born again*. Non-believers do not believe in life after death. For them death has the last word. Christians, though, believe that Jesus actually entered into the domain of death but was raised from the dead, thereby defeating death and opening the way to life eternal for all who believe in him. Unbelievers perhaps are satisfied with nothing past this life. I honestly believe that I would be a Christian even if there were no life after death simply because I believe that Jesus' way of life is far superior to any other. But it certainly is an added bonus to believe that he, not death, has the last word, that there is the hope of eternal life with him and the hope of reunion with loved ones. Coming to that hope does make life so different that it is like being born all over again.

125

So, being born again is not always a dramatic overpowering experience, though it can be. A friend of mine read very carefully about the conversion of C. S. Lewis in *Surprised by Joy* and discovered that the final step in the lengthy conversion process of that spiritual giant took place while Lewis was riding on the top of a double-decker bus. Lewis relates,

I know very well when, but hardly how, the final step was taken. I was driven to Whipsnade one sunny morning. When we set out I did not believe that Jesus Christ is the Son of God, and when we reached the zoo I did.[30]

Being born again is also not becoming morally perfect though it is marked by personal and spiritual growth. It is simply the sudden — or gradual, as was the case with many of us, including C. S. Lewis — experience of becoming aware of God's love for us in Jesus, realizing his forgiveness of our sin, reaching out in love to others, and being assured of life eternal.

The New Jerusalem Bible, the New American Bible, and other versions use a phrasing which may provide additional insight: "*No one can see the Kingdom of God without being born from above.*" The awareness of God's love and his other gifts comes to us from "above," from God and not by our own efforts. If that is the case, then the question remains, is there nothing that we can do to make the experience come to us?

For an answer we can ponder these words of Jesus:

Do not be surprised because I tell   you "You must all be born again." The wind blows wherever it wishes; you hear the sound it makes, but you do not know where it comes from or where it is going.   It is the same way with everyone who is born of the Spirit.   John 3:7,8

The clue is in the word *wind*, the biblical word for spirit.   In Genesis we read that when God created Adam, God *breathed life-giving breath* [or wind] *into his nostrils and the man began to live.* At Pentecost the Spirit came to the disciples like a mighty blowing wind.   We find throughout the scripture God's Spirit blowing about, touching people and events.

We cannot see the wind, but we can see its effects and feel its force. We know places and times the wind has blown before, so if we want to experience the wind, we can be present at those places and times.

We know that God blows his life-giving Spirit into the hearts of people in worship and prayer, in the sacraments and in service. If we are present on such occasions and if we watch and wait, his Spirit will come to us.   He will come with his love and his forgiveness with opportunities to love others.   He will come with his promise of life eternal. When we accept these gifts of God, our lives will be so different that it will be like being born all over again.

127

NOTES

[1] Chuck Swindoll, *The Quest for Character* (Portland: Multnomah Press, 1987), 26.

[2] Joe Elmore, *This Fleeting Instant* (Pensacola: Ardara House, 1993), 27.

[3] Walter Underwood, *Being Human Being Hopeful* (Nashville: Abingdon Press, 1987), 66.

[4] Paul Tournier, *The Adventure of Living* (New York: Harper & Row, 1965), 116.

[5] Cecil Osborne, *Release From Fear and Anxiety* (Waco: Word Books, 1976), 12.

[6] Swindoll, *Come Before Winter* (Portland: Multnomah Press, 1985), 96.

[7] Linus Mundy, *Prayer-Walking* (St. Meinrad: Abbey Press, 1994), 19,20.

[8] Tournier, *The Adventure of Living*, 216,217.

[9] Andrew Delbanco and Thomas Delbanco, "A.A. at the Crossroads," *New Yorker, 20 Mar. 1995: 52.*

[10] Nick Stinnet and John DeFran, *Family Building, Six Qualities of Strong Families,* ed. Dr. George Rakers (Ventura: Regal Books, 1985), 38.

[11] Tony Campolo, *Carpe Diem* (Dallas: Word Publishing, 1994), 175.

[12] Lewis B. Smedes, *Love Within Limits* (Grand Rapids: Eerdmans, 1978), 28.

[13] M. Scott Peck, *The Road Less Traveled* (New York: Simon and Schuster, 1978), 15.

[14] Stephen Covey, *The Seven Habits of Highly Effective People* (New York: Simon and Schuster, 1989), 83.

[15] Tom Verducci, "The High Price of Hard Living," *Sports Illustrated,* 27 Feb. 1995: 16-35.

[16] David H. C. Read, "It's All Imagination" (New York: Madison Avenue Presbyterian Church, Unpublished Sermon, delivered May 5, 1985).

[17] Read, "It's All Imagination"

[18] James Allen, *As A Man Thinketh* [This little book is out of copyright but is available in many editions. It is a good gift to give to recent high school and college graduates].

[19] Paul Klebnikov, "An Interview with Aleksandr Solzhenitsyn," *Forbes,* 9 May 1994: 118-122.

[20] Lloyd J. Ogilvie, *Ask Him Anything* (Waco: Word Books, 1984), 37,38.

[21] Leslie Weatherhead, *The Will of God* (Nashville: Abingdon Press, 1976).

[22] Harry E. Fosdick, *Riverside Sermons* (New York: Harper & Bros., 1958), 75.

[23] Swindoll, *Come Before Winter*, 72,73.

[24] Dietrich Bonhoeffer, *Life Together* (New York: Harper and Row, 1954), 112-113.

[25] Osborne, *You're In Charge* (Waco: Word Books, 1973), 39,40.

[26] Smedes, *Forgive and Forget* (San Francisco: Harper and Row, 1987) 75.

[27] Smedes, 76.

[28] Doris Donnelly, *Learning to Forgive* (New York: Macmillan, 1979), 32,54.

[29] E. Stanley Jones, *Abundant Living* (Nashville: Abingdon Press, 1942), 59.

[30] C. S. Lewis, *Surprised by Joy* (New York: Harcourt, Brace and World, 1955), 237.